SPECTRE 07

Memoir of a Risk-Taker

LIEUTENANT COLONEL ROBERT RENEAU, USAF, RETIRED

i

DEDICATION

I dedicate this book to Dottie, that wonderful loving, faithful, and tolerant "ace kicking" wife of forty-three years, who gave me her full backing, understanding, and two fine sons and six grandchildren.

I would also like to dedicate this memoir to the memory of my dear parents whom I think justly deserve credit (or blame) for the genetics and environment that gave me such an adventurist personality.

I also dedicate this to my wonderful sons and daughters; their children and grandchildren who carry my genes.

To all my progeny: if you find yourself feeling frisky and risky, I will gladly take the blame and recommend you follow through. Live your life to its fullest. It is for you that I have provided this limited historical account.

Since I did not write this memoir for the purpose of selling it, I will take this opportunity to make my personal tribute to the one to whom this book is truly dedicated, my "Ace Kicking" lover of 43 years.

The following poem is an amateurish attempt at writing poetry and was read at Dottie's funeral.

TO DOTTIE

When tomorrow starts without you
And you I cannot see,
I'll gaze upon your pillow
Where you used to lie with me.

My heart will still remind me
Of the way things used to be.
We loved, we laughed; we lived the life
That all our friends envy.

We traveled all around the world
And did such wondrous things
We danced and skied and sailed our boats
And really had our flings.

We raised two boys together,
Both strong and fair and tall.
We knew that as a family
We could match up with them all.

We played, we coached; we cheered them on
Through any sport around.
We taught them all our values
And they never let us down.

They grew to be outstanding
In all their many roles,
As pilots, husbands, fathers,
They attained our prayed-for goals.

And now, we three must carry on
Through life's trials, we'll survive,
Because, we know our wife and mother
Will be right there by our side.

Love, *Bob*

CONTENTS

ACKNOWLEDGMENTS

Due to my increasing age and complete lack of computer knowledge and photography, I am truly indebted to the following individuals.

Anita Laymon, serving as my editor and publishing expert.
Anita's grandson, Carson LaBo, for his expertise in photo editing.
Frank Aycock, for his initial editing, suggestions, and proofreading.
Rob Reneau, Mariah Reneau, and Joan Vasbinder for their computer assistance.
Rick Reneau, and Judy Geary for their encouragement and valuable suggestions.
Judy Milner, whose support and administrative skills are dearly appreciated.
Many members of the High Country Writers group for their encouragement and promises to read the finished book. (Note: they didn't promise to buy it.)
Thanks to Betsy and Al Brantley for their encouragement and suggestions A special thanks to Betsy for her portrait drawing of me shown on the back cover of this book.

SPECTRE 07
Memoir of a Risk-Taker

FORWARD

For many years, folks who have enjoyed my annual Christmas letters have commented that I should write a book. I have also received requests from my children and grandchildren to fill out those little commercial booklets asking my favorite colors, my hobbies, my first girlfriend, etc.

I recently re-read a biography (non-published) written by my father which gives a somewhat detailed history of his life. He neglected to

My dad, somewhere in France after coming ashore on Omaha Beach

spend much time on his experiences in World War II where he served as a chaplain who went ashore at Omaha Beach during the D-Day invasion. When his landing craft was blown out of the water, he made it ashore on a drifting pontoon. He was in the Battle of the Bulge and many other significant battles. He shared many memories of that war with my brother and me. Sadly, he neglected to write about his experiences.

A dear friend at church recently recognized the Silver Star military decoration I usually wear on my lapel. She encouraged me to tell her about my war experiences. I shared with her a letter I had recently written to a young man whose father had been a navigator on the AC-130 during the Vietnam War. This young man asked if I could shed some light on the mission as he was planning to write a book on the gunship. My friend was enthralled by the subject, and insisted that I share it with my children and grandchildren. Others in my life also have had questions about my experiences.

I have decided to respond to all those requests with only one caveat: I am writing this book solely for providing information for my children and grandchildren, hopefully in a format that will hold their interest. Any others that might get access to this document can read it at their own risk as it might seem somewhat boring to non-relatives. It will probably seem boring to some relatives.

Therefore, this will be an autobiography of an unimportant man (except to my progeny). If you are one of those, you will probably have to go to your dictionary (excuse me, your Wikipedia, nowadays) to look up the word *progeny*. (I know I did) I will pause while you do that...

Because we all know that the appendix is a non-vital or unnecessary organ in anatomy, I will possibly provide some of those unnecessary organs in this offering, which can be read at the discretion, age, and interest level of the reader. Then again, possibly not.

Some of you non-related folks should probably go to chapter 9 about my AC-130 experiences, as they are probably the most interesting. If you are interested in finding the source of the title of this autobiography, you will find the answer in the same chapter. I am also going to introduce a somewhat different format from most books, in that I will rely on flashbacks in an attempt to keep it somewhat interesting by combining my history in a not-so-chronological presentation.

CHAPTER 1

An Ace in the Hole (almost)

I've really got it made, working with NASA on the Eastern Test Range here in Florida. It sure as hell beats the three years I spent in Southeast Asia working my ass off trying to make the world "safe for democracy."

February has always been one of my favorite months in Florida. Raised in Oklahoma, I had grown to despise the hot months of summer and the frigid winter months when "the wind comes sweeping down the plain" and seemed to bite through every layer of clothing my mom could convince me to wear. Now I've found paradise. Here I can swim almost year-round. I get to fly to Johannesburg, South Africa, almost every other month and take trips around the world supporting the Gemini space program. I am wondering, what is a small town kid from Sapulpa, Oklahoma, doing on a beachside tennis court at Patrick Air Force Base with a beautiful girl across the net who has just served her third straight ace of the game?

My beautiful "Ace Kicking" wife

I met Dottie on a blind date. She was supposed to have been a blond. I fell for her right away, and when she asked if I liked tennis, I lied and said I loved it. (I hadn't picked up a tennis racquet since the seventh grade.)

She gives me a 'just-you-wait' grin as she walks off the court to tend to the pacifier that fell from our son's stroller tray. Her demeanor seemed to say, "Take that you chauvinistic hunk of manliness." The answer is coming through quite clearly. Dottie has developed a pang of conscience and has given me a short respite before delivering her final thrust of vengeance for several weeks of leaving her to the dirty diapers of our one-year-old son Robbie.

"I love you dearly," she says, "but a girl's got to do what a girl's got to do." I can tell she is also a little pissed with the mess of changing diapers for the wonderful Valentine present I had given her - an eighteen month old Basset Hound named Mandy who had managed to come into heat just prior to my last trip to Johannesburg. I guess I am getting off pretty lucky, so what's one more deftly delivered ace to my backhand corner.

I guess if that's my only problem in this world in late February of 1968 then what the hell. "I know where you're coming from," I say, partly in jest and partly in true fear. I deftly cover my ass with my racquet as I bend over to retrieve the previously mentioned ace. I know what this beautiful wife of mine is capable of if she sets her mind to providing me with the other two balls so that I can take serve. (Her tennis coach at Holiday Park in Fort Lauderdale had been Jimmy Evert, Chris Evert's Dad.)

Bending over in this somewhat convoluted position, I notice Bill Olsen crossing the street toward the court. He has one of those looks of anticipation on his face that lets you know something is about to happen. Bill is one of those "little old lady" (wrapped in safety and regulations) types of pilots. He is the unit's flying safety officer, and although he doesn't have nearly the flying experience that most of us have, he feels it is his responsibility to ensure that everyone dots their i's and crosses their t's, (which is his responsibility when it comes to flying safety).

Obviously, I am somewhat concerned by the look on his face. I can just imagine that someone has reported the low-level buzz job I had delivered on Mauritius Island last week at the request of the hotel owner where we stay when we are flying in the Indian Ocean. He always asks us to pass the hotel low enough to blow up some thatch on the hotel roof for the pleasure of his martini-sipping hotel guests whom he would have gathered on the seaside veranda.

We had obliged him when we returned from retrieving the telemetry capsules by snagging them from the down range telemetry ships with davit poles extending down from our ramp and door. The pole had hooks to grab a harness around a blimp-like balloon. The balloon was tethered by a special 200-foot stretchable rope tied to a capsule on the ship's deck. We would then wench them up and into the aircraft using the All American Recovery System. The capsules contained the telemetry (data) transmitted from orbiting space vehicles and standard rocket launches from Cape Kennedy.

"Guess what guys" he says, "I just found out that I got orders to Thailand."

"Whew," I thought; "what a relief." Not that he was leaving, but that he hadn't come over to chew my ass out about the buzz job in Mauritius.

Bill and I had come to Patrick AFB from Okinawa together, and had been here almost three years. The Vietnam War has been heating up, and we have heard rumors that they will be taking our aircraft to modify into AC-130 Gunships. Although I haven't told Dottie, I'm not too surprised that they are going to be moving some of us out.

Bill isn't a high time 130 pilot, nor is he an instructor pilot, so I am a little surprised when he announces that he is going to be one of the six initial AC-130 pilots.

I must admit that I am just a little jealous, as that would be an ideal assignment if I had to go back. However, I have been married to that ace kicking tennis player for less than two years, and our lives are really taking off, what with that one-year-old imp and the vacation-like lifestyle we are enjoying.

I feel good for Bill, and I am glad it is he and not I. I do, however, notice the "there is more to the story" look on Bill's face. He then proceeds to announce, "Someone else from the base has also been selected to be in the initial cadre for the Gunship program," he said. Then it hit me.

Bill is not a tennis fan, nor is he particularly fond of one-year-old babies. If he didn't make the trip out here to chew my ass out about the buzz job, there had to be another reason for this intrusion, ill-timed as it was. "You're going, too," he said.

Talk about the horns of a dilemma. Do I express elation at the opportunity and risk the extreme wrath of my somewhat vindictive lover, or do I piss and moan reflecting poorly on my understanding of duty as an Air Force Officer. The second choice made in front of an individual who is superior to me in rank, and one with whom I will be serving for the next year, didn't seem acceptable either. Discretion being the better part of valor, and realizing that my beloved is almost in tears and is clutching that somewhat weapon-like tennis racquet, I am quite relieved to find myself speechless.

This was obviously the end of a lop-sided tennis match, and the beginning of a long tear-filled walk home, not to mention the beginning of who knows what: the end of my life in a fireball in some Asian jungle, or the most exciting and unforgettable year in my life. This is not the first time in my life where I was excited about new and somewhat dangerous adventures. Let me take you back to my childhood.

CHAPTER 2

The Risk-taker

I realize that I have been a risk-taker since I was very young. My folks tell stories of me slipping away from home and venturing all over town on my tricycle when I was three years old. I guess I was lucky that Watonga, Oklahoma, is a very small town. They would tell of me riding my tricycle to the local movie theatre, where I would park it outside and enter to enjoy the movie. The staff would notify Mom that I had arrived again and that they would ensure I was OK.

The same stunt would take me over to the local elementary school where I would just enter the classroom and sit down. The principal would call Mom with the same result. (I find it hard to believe that I would climb out the window to go to a school). The movie, I can understand. The big difference is that I still love movies, but school is another matter.

My earliest risk taking adventures

Let me explain the window escape opportunities. It got very hot in Oklahoma in 1940, and there was no such thing as air conditioning, so the windows were always open. Screen locks were very easy to figure out.

The one escapade I personally remember about those times was when I decided to tie a cowbell to a rope and just toss it over the clothesline. (Yep, no automatic washing machines or dryers either.) This was not a very good idea. I still carry the scar on my forehead where the cowbell hit me when it returned after it reached its maximum radius after crossing over the clothesline.

As I got a little older, (probably six years) I continued taking risks. I think I was asked to leave at least two kindergarten schools for some "alleged" behavior problems. I say alleged only if you think that pulling the children's chair out from under a somewhat portly teacher when she attempted to sit with us around the worktable as being a behavioral problem.

I don't remember the event in the other situation, but I'm sure my mother could have told you, if her reaction to the chair pulling episode is any indication of her tolerance level. Let me remind you that this was during an era where corporal punishment in schools was an acceptable form of punishment, and punishment at home was also allowed and not considered child abuse.

As I recall, there were several other instances of corporal punishment being administered to yours truly in and out of school while I was developing my loving and tolerant personality. I would probably be described in today's terms as a borderline ADD child. If not, that's my excuse, and I'm sticking to it. At least it gives me something on which to blame some of my overactive childhood experiences.

I might add here that I started taking risks (although somewhat entrepreneurial) at a very young age. I had my first fulltime job at the age of eight, delivering the Lawton (Oklahoma) Constitution in Walters, Oklahoma. At the same age, I also had a part time job at the local slaughterhouse plucking turkeys. I made 15 cents for a hen and 25 cents for a tom. After they slit the turkey's throats and dragged them through scalding water, we would walk around following an overhead assembly line in the ceiling that was weaving around the room like a Disney World waiting line. We had to be sure and be finished plucking by the end of the line, or we were docked some pay, and someone else would finish the bird. I remember wanting to be that person, because they didn't have to walk all around the room on the hard concrete floor.

Occasionally we kids would get a break when a turkey broke loose and flew out the back of the loading dock prior to getting it's throat cut. I remember having mixed emotions about whether I preferred to chase and wrestle a frantic turkey to the ground, or to climb a nearby tree where a turkey had come to roost. I think I preferred the chasing and wrestling to the tree climbing. Climbing the tree wasn't too bad, but climbing back down with one hand groping for limbs to keep from falling, and the other hand grasping a highly pissed off turkey with flapping wings tugging him through the leaves and branches was no fun at all. They did pay us a small stipend for our daring-do.

I might mention here that at the age of nine, I played trumpet in the Walters High School band. You'll know how small Walters was, because the high school football team's quarterback would put on a raincoat at halftime and join the band to play trumpet as well.

The following spring, we moved to Raton, New Mexico where I continued my entrepreneurial pursuits. By now, I was in the 5th grade, and continued with a full time paper route for the Raton Range.

I also started several other small business projects: a window washing business and a seasonal leaf-raking and snow-shoveling company. I worked for a photography studio color-tinting sepia portraits. In the holiday season, I solicited Christmas tree orders from neighbors, and then went into the local mountains, cutting trees and dragging them home. I made Christmas tree stands out of two boards and wire. I worked as a pinsetter for a local bowling alley. I worked on a farm loading hay for the winter, and for a funeral director delivering and setting up memorial flower wreaths at local churches. The funeral director owned a beautiful Paint (brown and white for those who don't know horse breeds), which I was allowed to ride and exercise on a regular basis.

One of my unusual jobs was selling popcorn, peanuts, and corn dogs at the local para-mutual betting race track at Raton. It's not that being a grandstand hustler at a race track was unusual, but the fact that the races were on Sunday afternoon, and that I was the son of the pastor of the first Methodist church in Raton, and all of the locals knew it.

One terrible experience I had there was witnessing the results of a Sunday morning stable fire in which many of the thoroughbred racehorses were burned to death. Those damaged horses not killed were being euthanized as I arrived, and the carcasses were lying all around the area.

Another unusual job was that of a dining room worker. What made the job unusual was that I worked in a tent. Every year when the circus came to town, we kids would race to the setup site to get menial jobs. I think that because I wasn't big enough to drive stakes setting up tents, I was selected to serve as wait-staff in the performers' and workers' dining tent. I learned that most of the laborers preferred to eat their cereal with water instead of milk. I remember that to this day, and have occasionally put that knowledge to good use when in a situation or country where milk was not available, or not recommended to drink. For that matter neither was the water in some countries. However, wine could serve as an interesting substitution. No, I never put wine on my cereal.

In Raton, the high school was located with the junior high. While I was still in junior high, I had the opportunity to play in and march with the high school band as well as sing with the high school chorus.

Two other vivid memories of this period were the death of a fifth grade schoolmate from pneumonia. I had a crush on her and visited her from the sidewalk outside the hospital, since she had a first floor room with a window to the sidewalk and she couldn't have visitors. I might add an interesting aspect to this story: There was another classmate who also had a crush on her. He even picked a fight with me over her.

One other aspect to this story is about my rescue of a drowning student in the high school indoor pool. The PE teacher/coach had already left the pool area when a fellow student who was a non-swimmer yelled out, "Edward is down there," pointing to the bottom of the pool. I was a good swimmer; I hit the water from the opposite side of the pool. I had the student to the surface when the PE teacher, who had been alerted by the other students, returned and helped me get Edward out of the pool. The interesting aspect of the story is that Edward is the classmate who picked the fight with me over our mutual girlfriend. Edward didn't require artificial respiration, but I got my butt chewed out by the PE teacher/coach for risking my life. Later in life, as a lifeguard at many pools, I had to rescue several swimmers, but that butt chewing stayed with me to this day.

During high school, I worked as a lifeguard at two swimming pools, one in Sapulpa, and the other at the Southern Hills Country Club in Tulsa. I had to hitchhike every day (twenty miles each way) to work at Southern Hills Country Club. Also in Sapulpa, I worked as an usher and ticket taker at the Yale Theatre and at the local drive-in theatre. I was a "drug dealer" (read "distributer") for a local drug store. I would ride my bike all over town delivering prescriptions to local residents. One summer I worked as a maintenance man at Frankoma pottery in Sapulpa.

Those acts of risk-taking didn't end as I "matured" (a term I use with some trepidation). As I got older I was a pole-vaulter, football fullback, 3-meter diver, clown diver, Air Force combat pilot, football coach, soccer coach, and probably the riskiest of endeavors, being soccer referee and real estate broker.

Let me go into some depth on my sports escapades. As a youth and a competitive swimmer, I represented Sapulpa High School as the entire team at the Oklahoma High School Championship. I was swimming the 100 yd. freestyle final. There was a false start, but there was no false start rope and I made it all the way to the end of the pool and part way back before someone jumped in to stop me. They were nice enough to give me a two minute rest before the restart. I finished high, but didn't win. I still maintain that I am the reigning 76-yard Oklahoma swimming champion.

I was also the pole-vaulter on the Sapulpa High track squad. I qualified at the conference and district level and made it to the State championship at the University of Oklahoma in Norman. I had been using an old steel pole, and had no way to transport it to Norman. My coach arranged for me to travel to the meet with the large Tulsa Central High School team. They had a new Swedish steel flexible pole that I could

Pole vaulter at SMU

use. I had tried one on a couple of occasions so I agreed to compete using their pole. On my first attempt at 10 ft., the pole snapped, sending me under the bar to an embarrassing landing in the sawdust pit. Apparently, someone had dropped a large steel shot, used in the shot put competition, onto the pole, creasing it enough to snap on me. That ended my competition.

My best vault of my career was 11 feet 6 inches, which isn't very high by today's standards, but the equipment has changed drastically since those days. The Rev. Bob Richards held the Olympic record of just under 15 feet, set in 1952. My performance was good enough to make the Southern Methodist University freshman track team. In those days, freshmen could not compete on the varsity teams. That was OK, as I had come to SMU on a swimming and diving scholarship, and dropped pole-vaulting.

I am not politically involved, and in fact, I am currently registered as a "Nonaffiliated" or "Independent." I don't know how it is today, but in my day, military officers were dissuaded from expressing political views, if we had them. However, I did have a go at politics in High School. I ran for and was elected to the office of President of the Sapulpa High School Student Council, and the Vice President of the Youth Board. I'm happy to announce that there were no assassination attempts or political protests during my tenure as President.

Starting Fullback 1955
Sapulpa High School

Before leaving my high school adventures, I should mention my football career. I didn't play varsity football until my junior year. Prior to that, I was a member of the high school band where I played first chair trombone. As it turned out, I was the starting fullback on the football team in my senior year, and was the leading scorer and ground gainer. I didn't get to play in the last game against Tulsa Central because I had suffered a concussion in the previous game against Muscogee, one of the best teams in

22

the state. We played in the 4A division, which at that time was the highest football division. I know that my sons will say that the concussion accounts for some of my questionable personality.

A college scout from the University of Oklahoma asked me if I would be interested in playing college football. That was during the reign of Bud Wilkinson, and I would have probably been squashed to death just sitting on the bench of the national championship team, since I only weighed 155 lbs. Besides, I already had been offered a swimming scholarship to SMU. I was told that there were four girls to each guy at SMU, and most of them were very well off.

As a swimmer and diver at SMU, I was recruited by the American Red Cross to participate in their water safety show at the Texas State Fair in Dallas in 1957. In addition to diving in the safety show, they asked me to be a clown diver. I always thought my straight diving was pretty funny in and of itself. I agreed and had a great time until I hit my head on the bottom of the pool requiring a few stitches.

Practicing diving for the Red Cross water safety show at Texas State Fair

I might add that I hadn't lost that entrepreneurial spirit. Between the shows, I worked as a Chinese coolie wearing a Chinese hat and pulling tourists around the Texas State Fair Grounds in a gin rickshaw.

I'm the clown in the hat

You might say that I continued my risk-taking in college. During the summer vacation after my freshman year, a friend named Richard Jones and I decided to hitchhike from Ponca City, Oklahoma, to Houston, Texas, to see my freshman girlfriend. The hitchhiking was successful, if you consider speeding down an east Texas highway in the back seat with two bearded "good old boys" in the front seat drinking beer being completely successful. Yet, the entire trip was somewhat less than successful due to the fact that the wealthy father of that freshman girlfriend wasn't overly impressed with two Oklahoma Sooners having to hitchhike across two states to see his daughter. He did, however, let us stay in his guest house overnight, and we were on our way the next morning. Oh well, not all risks pay off as planned.

There are a few things I should mention about my college days. Prior to my junior year, I had met a young lady from my dad's church in Ponca

Southwest Conference 400 yd. Freestyle Relay Champions, 1958
Left to right: Bob Reneau, Steve Mulholland, Dick Rantzow, Mike Lumby

City, Oklahoma. We were married in 1957, and our first daughter, Cindy, was born just before my graduation in 1959.

While at SMU, I was involved in varsity swimming, lettering all three years, and a member of the Southwest Conference championship team all three years. The Southwest Conference consisted of the University of Texas, Texas A&M, SMU, Rice, TCU, the University of Arkansas, and Baylor.

In my senior year I was also the cadet commander of the Air Force ROTC. I was a member of the Phi Delta Theta fraternity. In the group were Don Meredith "Dandy Don", quarterback of the Dallas Cowboys and Monday night football commentator along with Howard Cosell, and Frank Gifford. Don Meredith was my little brother in the fraternity; he used my fraternity pin to pin his first wife. (I don't know if they still do that.)

While at SMU, I worked at several jobs in addition to the State Fair Red Cross demonstrations. I worked several jobs in the summer, most of which were back at Ponca City. The first long hot summer, I worked for a lumber yard, delivering lumber to work projects. I had a commercial driver's license. That was the best part of the job. The rest of the day was spent stacking lumber, unloading boxcar loads of lumber, sheetrock and the most dreaded, bags of cement. Believe me, those boxcars were very uncomfortable in the intense Oklahoma summer heat.

I wised up and my next few summer jobs were as a lifeguard at the country club and city pool. After getting married, my jobs were in Dallas. One job was as a youth counselor at Highland Park United Methodist Church. Another job was at a local J.J. Boyd appliance store selling air conditioners, TVs, and other appliances.

CHAPTER 3

Becoming an Officer and a "Gentleman"

I had to emphasize the word, "gentleman," because on many occasions I needed to mention to doubting individuals that I was in fact a gentleman as verified by the President of the United States on my commissioning certificate. I might note that the term is no longer used in that there are now commissioned ladies and, if the truth were known, the term was sometimes greatly exaggerated, especially in my day, which included the Vietnam war.

Me as a New "Butter bar"

I graduated in May, the same month our daughter Cindy was born, as a "distinguished Graduate and commissioned Regular Officer." I was selected to enter pilot training immediately to compete with the first Air Force Academy graduates. We always joked that since the academics in pilot training were graded on the curve, meaning that someone had to fail, we were recruited as "cannon fodder."

I did my pilot training at two bases in Texas. My primary training was at Moore AB in Mission, Texas, and basic training at Webb AFB in Big Spring, Texas. I was involved in a couple of interesting occurrences in pilot training.

The first one occurred at Moore AB. This is a true story (as all of mine are). My Aunt Ruth who lived in Boston, Massachusetts, told me she read about it in a paper up there.

We were the first class to fly the brand new T-37 twin jet trainer. (Both of my sons also flew it at pilot training, and both said it was a real antique. "Getting old is sometimes harsh.") The T-37 had a clamshell canopy made of Plexiglas that opened like a convertible top. On my solo flight (first flight without an instructor), we were going to our auxiliary field "Tamale," the name and call sign. My instructor for this flight was the assistant flight commander Mr. Moore. Our flight commander Mr. Tyson, was there staffing the auxiliary control tower, or in this case "shack." His job was to monitor proper gear and flap settings on landing aircraft, and maintain constant radio contact with students in the pattern area.

We were never told when we were going to solo, so it could come as a surprise. After a couple of landings with Mr. Moore, he said to pull off the runway where he proceeded to get out of the aircraft. This meant that I was to make my first solo flight.

I closed the clamshell canopy, and taxied out for takeoff. On my departure just after liftoff, my clamshell canopy started to open. This would be like driving on the interstate in a convertible and the canvas roof begin to open. I took my hand off the throttle and attempted to lock the canopy with my elbow (which I had obviously neglected to do prior to takeoff). As the airspeed increased because of leveling off, I was committed to continue, holding the canopy on with both hands. Now who's steering this twin engine jet? Well, I am, of course, with my feet off the rudders and the control stick between my legs. Taking a chance, I held the canopy with one hand long enough to reduce the power to the point I could fly with one hand and both feet on the rudders.

Being the well-trained aspiring pilot, I called the control shack to report the situation. No answer, so I attempted to contact "Sunbath" our big control tower back at Moore field, no answer there either. I decided to continue in the pattern, switching my hands between holding the canopy, the control stick, and the throttles. I definitely couldn't fly the normal 180 degree overhead pitch-out pattern so I elected to fly a normal base-to-final pattern. I was continually trying to make radio contact with the control shack or the main tower at Moore AB. I even went on guard channel and transmitted "Mayday, Mayday." I needed to land at Tamale. By then, I was pretty much lined up on final and had slowed my airspeed so I decided to try once again to lock the canopy with my elbow. It worked!! Meanwhile, Mr. Tyson had come back into the control shack, and not having checked my gear and flaps with his binoculars, he said "T-37 on final, take it around." I said, "this is Blackjack 50 (my call sign), and I need to land." He said "Blackjack 50, take it around (meaning make another pattern and approach), there is a declared emergency in the area." Now that I pretty much had most everything under control, I thought that there must be another emergency trying to land, maybe even a B-47 from Dyess AFB was on fire and needed to land, so I took it around. As it turned out, the other emergency in the area turned out to be me, because I had transmitted the "Mayday" call.

I made a normal landing and taxied to the spot where I had dropped off Mr. Moore and opened that "damn canopy." As he was crawling in over the side he said, and I quote, "Damn, it's a good thing you weren't with me." My answer was "Damn, it's a good thing you weren't with me either."

He explained what happened to him. As he was walking from my aircraft to the control shack to watch my performance, a "large" Texas rattlesnake coiled and struck at him. Mr. Tyson in the control shack witnessed the attack, grabbed a shovel, and joined Mr. Moore in his "escape and evasion dance."

They obviously missed my radio pleas, and upon returning to the control shack, Mr. Tyson hadn't been able to visually check my landing gear and flap settings. Meanwhile, he had received a radio call from Moore tower that some aircraft in the vicinity had declared a "Mayday emergency." I then related my story, and he stated, "Damn, I don't know if either of us is calm enough to fly back to home base." He also declared that we each deserved a drink at the Officers Club. I immediately agreed. We were able to fly back to Moore AFB and yes, we went to the club for a drink, or two, or three. One thing I do remember is that the snake kept growing in length each time Mr. Moore related his daring escapade.

An interesting anecdote was that after the incident, Mr. Tyson, in his morning briefings, referred to me as 'Superman' for having the strength to hold the canopy down. It wasn't long after that that he announced at the briefing that "I will no longer refer to Lt. Reneau as "Superman," because I had the very same thing happen to me, and the canopy wasn't that heavy. I countered with, "That's not quite the same, as you had two pilots in the cockpit and therefore could use both hands." This drew laughter from the entire flight.

Two other experiences occurred at Moore AB. One involved an OSI (Office of Special Investigation) investigation into broken glass discovered in the club pool after a squadron party. I wasn't involved in the incident, but was called in and interviewed by the OSI. Another memory is my debut as a standup comedian at a squadron party. I no longer do standup comedy.

Another incident occurred at Webb AFB in Big Spring, Texas. My instructor and I were returning from an overnight cross-country mission to Las Vegas, Nevada. In route home, we lost all electrical power in the T-33 (the single engine jet aircraft used for basic training). We were briefed that the weather was deteriorating as forecasted, but once into the weather and committed to land at Webb without electrical power, we had no instrumentation or radios to divert or make an approach. My instructor elected to descend in the weather to try to pick up a highway, or something else to perform "dead reckoning" navigation, using visual sightings.

By the time we landed at Webb AFB, we had received four FAA violations. The four included buzzing the town of Big Springs, buzzing the Cosden Oil refinery in Big Springs, buzzing Webb Air Force Base, and landing without permission. (Remember, we had no radios and our battery was dead due to a bad cockpit closing cutoff switch the night before, leaving us with a very low, non-recharging battery). Upon learning of our plight after landing, all violations were dropped, and we were actually commended for getting the aircraft back and not ejecting.

CHAPTER 4

Sewart AFB., Tennessee

My first assignment out of pilot training was to Sewart AFB, Tennessee. I only spent 18 months there, but they were very important months in my Air Force career development. Our second daughter, Karen, was born there in Murfreesboro, Tennessee.

Upon arrival, we contracted for an under-construction brick 3 bedroom and 1½ bath house with garage. It's hard to believe but we only paid $14,000 for it. Seems so cheap, but my base pay as a 2ⁿᵈ Lt. was $222.00 per month plus $100.00 flight pay and less than $100.00 for the food and clothing allowance. We did get a small housing supplement for living off base, but I can't remember what it amounted to. After all, I think I'm doing quite well for an 80-year-old in remembering anything.

As a 2ⁿᵈ Lt., I was a co-pilot on the brand new C-130 Hercules. We flew the A-models in the 314ᵗʰ Troop Carrier Wing. The first C-130 A models came out in 1953, so our oldest birds were only 7 years old. The other wing, the 463ʳᵈ TCW, flew the newer B-models.

During the time at Sewart I spent a lot of time away from home and four months TDY (Temporary Duty) to Evreux AB in France. From there, we spent a good deal of the time flying all over Europe and the Middle East as NATO resources. I have about four or five interesting missions to relate.

Flying into Teheran, the capital of Iran, we blew a tire on landing. Maintenance support was far away and we found it would be several days before they could get us a new tire. Therefore, we had to stay in a hotel. On the way to the hotel, we noticed armored tanks assembling at many street corners. Upon arrival at the hotel, we were advised not to leave the hotel, since there was a revolution starting against the current Shah.

Most of members of our five-man crew were smart enough to obey the advice, but our loadmaster couldn't resist going out to see the city. Unfortunately, he got stoned. It was not in the sense of having too much to drink, but really stoned. The crowds started throwing rocks at him. Fortunately, he was able to evade them and run back to the hotel. The embassy decided it wasn't safe enough for us to remain at the hotel, and secretly hustled us out of the city to a plush mountain retreat lodge, complete with swimming pool.

We later learned that our new abode was a special lodge maintained for Iranian high ranking officers and officials to rest and enjoy the pleasantries of beautiful female companions (if you get my drift). That place would have made Dolly Parton proud to shoot a movie entitled "The Best Little Whore House in Iran" at that location. Fortunately, it had outlived its use as such before we arrived. We spent about four days luxuriating before the darn support maintenance unfortunately showed up with a new tire.

A second mission took us to Peshawar, Pakistan, in support of our US reconnaissance mission. It was from this base that Gary Francis Powers flew his now-famous U-2 mission. Upon arrival, we were transported to the base in the back of an open bed stake truck. On the way, the local townspeople threw water at us. Not being up to speed on local customs, we reported it to the base authorities only to learn that it was a friendly gesture and not one of protest of our arrival. It was a local custom, as I learned is common in many Asian countries when a country is experiencing a drought. Because the locals can't afford to provide drinks for weary road travelers, they throw small amounts of water on them in hopes of appealing to the gods to end the drought.

Another interesting trip was to Dhahran Saudi Arabia, Asmara Ethiopia, and Athens, (Glyfada) Greece, where we were diverted to Wheelus Air Base, Libya (not on the original schedule) before returning to Evreux AB, France. This was a mission to remember.

The mission was on the schedule as the 101 mission. It was a favorite of the crews at Evreux, as it covered so many countries. The trip to Dhahran was uneventful, but the rest was memorable. I was the co-pilot on this trip. The first night, our aircraft commander started complaining about pains in his chest, but refused to alert medical authorities. (I think for fear of being retained in Saudi Arabia.) He felt OK in the morning and we continued our mission to Asmara, Ethiopia, to pick up a load of vegetables for the base.

Asmara is located high in the mountainous, somewhat coastal area. Ethiopian laborers loaded our aircraft based on the warehouse weights. Unannounced to us, they had been left outside in the rain overnight, and had gained a tremendous amount of weight. Several factors -- the high altitude, the temperature, the shorter runway, and that our takeoff data had not included the increased weight of the wet vegetables -- added to our predicament. On takeoff we went screaming toward the end of the runway. Fortunately for us, the runway ended at the beginning of a cliff, and the aircraft commander, Captain Nord, who had been recalled into the Air Force and was an experienced Burma Hump pilot, elected to continue the takeoff, as aborting the takeoff without knowing what effect the increased weight would have on our stopping distance, could have resulted in our going off the cliff. We had to dive down into the valley to build up our flying speed to remain airborne and continue the mission.

On our return mission from Dhahran to France, we were directed to stop in Athens to unload our regular cargo, and proceed to Wheelus Air Base in Libya. We were told to stand by on alert to go to the Congo to pick up Libyan troops. We were then to return the Libyan troops to Libya in order for them to prepare to invade France, where we were based. This was just one of the idiosyncrasies of being a NATO resource. We did not have to fly that mission, as the French, in their infinite wisdom, closed their airways and drove trucks onto their runways to deny landings to possible invading Libyans. We were now stuck in Libya on alert. After a few days, they took us off alert and we could lead our normal lives, but not return to France as the blockade was still in effect.

A C-124 (Old Shaky) crew returning from the Congo was also detained, and they just happened to have many cases of champagne that they had "liberated" from the Congo. They had nothing particular in mind as to how to dispose of it, since their return to France with it onboard, would possibly result in some customs problems. Being innovative and concerned about their possible customs problem, we decided to help them solve their problem (at least part of it).

We were in the midst of a great party when the AO (Airdrome Officer of the day) caught up with me, only to inform me that the French had decided to open their airways and runways for a limited time in order to recover all of the NATO aircraft. I expressed my concern as to our crew rest requirements and the obvious effects of our champagne consumption.

This was the only time in my career I was ordered to fly inebriated. I will say that flying while being slightly hung over might be a different matter. We found a large coffee urn with some cold coffee remaining in the bottom and proceeded to drink several cups. I think you know what drinking coffee while inebriated does to the system. Yep, wide awake drunks. That flight back to France from North Africa remains in my memory as the longest flight I can remember. Fortunately, the long flight afforded a chance to sober up before being required to make a weather approach to an almost Zero-Zero visibility landing.

Some of the squadron who had not been caught out on the routes due to the airfield closing, decided to celebrate (not having to fly for a while) by having a party. I might say here that fearing a possible land attack from local Libyan 'sympathetos' caused the Airbase authorities to set up a perimeter guard of enlisted airmen all around the base. Unfortunately, (or fortunately) they were issued M-1 rifles but no ammunition. They were there for appearance's sake only, but told not to interfere with any attempt to enter the base, since they didn't want to upset the French citizens.

Our crews lived on the opposite side of the runway from the main base. Some crewmembers had purchased old Citron sedans for the duration of our four-month TDY and a few of them decided to load up and drive around the rear perimeter road throwing cherry bomb fireworks. This resulted in the Air Police and OSI getting involved. Fortunately, I wasn't involved, as at the time we were trying to make a Zero-Zero (zero ceiling and zero visibility) landing. I have wondered at times, had I been there, would I have been involved. This was the infamous 50th Troop Carrier Squadron. Although some of us belonged to the 62nd Troop Carrier Squadron, we were on loan to the 50th.

On another flight, we got into weather on a trip from France to England. In the old A model C-130 we had to carry many VHF radio crystals to be inserted under the navigator's table. Different radio control stations used different crystals. On this particular flight, the English radar controllers requested crystals we didn't have on board. Failing to comply with their requests, they told us we were cleared to leave airways and radar control. We were in weather, and the aircraft commander elected to depart airways under VFR (Visual Flight Rules). This meant we were not offered flight-following radar, and had to remain clear of clouds and weather on our own. This was impossible due to our already being in the weather.

The pilot picked his way down, trying to avoid thunderstorms. We sighted a tall brick chimney as we approached some clear weather and stayed out of the weather using what they call dead reckoning -- following roads and highways -- trying to find an airfield at which to land. American bases use a split tower beacon to identify themselves. We found an unknown American Air Base, so we made a VFR approach and landed without clearance and without radio contact. Unknown to us, it happened to be a highly classified SAC base named Upper Heyford and we were met by a jeep with mounted 50-caliber machine guns aimed at our cockpit.

Many years later, I returned to Upper Heyford as the backfield coach and offensive coordinator for the European Conference champion Rhein Main Rockets football team. We were to play the Upper Heyford, United Kingdom championship team for the championship of the entire USAFE command. The reception after our victory was much like the one received after our unannounced arrival 10 years earlier, but much more enjoyable since we won the game. I might mention here that our head coach suffered chest pains at halftime in the locker room, and wasn't available for the second half. We won it anyway, and it was determined that the head coach had suffered from stress and was released from the hospital the next day.

One note in departing -- when we left Evreux to return to the United States we came back as a mixed squadron (as the rest of the 62nd TCS had joined with the 50th squadron), flying back to the US in corridor formation (15 minutes in trail of the preceding aircraft). The lead aircraft, upon takeoff, fired off his emergency flare gun as a departing shot. Our squadron operations officer warned each succeeding aircrew not to do the same. In the interest of protecting our lead aircraft commander, each and every succeeding aircraft fired off their flare guns, thus setting the runway infield on fire as an exclamation point ending to this episode!!

Upon our arrival back at Sewart AFB, our aircraft had to fly through a line of thunderstorms. We were struck by lightning, which cracked our Radome and knocked out our radio communication capability. The standard radio-out procedure is to make a pass down the runway and rock the wings to draw the attention of the tower. The runway buzz without rocking the wings was a symbol of bragging about your mission, (only allowed if approved by the tower). Obviously, without radios, we were unable to contact the tower. We were in for it until the authorities met our aircraft, and they noticed our cracked Radom. I can only say, "Those Were the Days." Those four-month TDY's (temporary duty) almost back–to-back between France and Panama resulted in many divorces. I am sure that it could become quite lonely for wives, staying back home with children, while their husbands were visiting interesting hot spots around the world for four months at a time.

My eighteen months at Sewart, which included the four months in France, provided many experiences and many flights across the Atlantic Ocean.

One mission, we launched 36 C-130's to Europe to participate in operation "Scrap Iron." This was to demonstrate to the Soviet Bloc countries our prowess and capabilities. We were dropping heavy equipment loads near the Russian/Turkish border. This meant two consecutive days of flying nine hours of tight formation in the V's in trail, and V of Vees (formation-flying like the symbol conveyed by geese in flight) formations each day. I was a young co-pilot and had a crusty veteran aircraft commander who took advantage of the second day of flying tight formation, by turning the formation flying over to me, while he slept in the left seat. This was somewhat due to the drinking party the night after the first mission. I was able to really hone my tight formation flying skills after the many hours of that flight. Was I about to awaken him? No way Jose'! That experience enabled me to become one of the best tight formation pilots around then and later on.

A side-light to that mission was the failure of the release mechanisms on the bottom of all the heavy equipment drop pallets containing jeeps and other wheeled vehicles. This failure resulted in the main parachutes remaining attached to the pallets, and, due to high winds, resulted in the pallets being flipped over, destroying the loaded vehicles.

That detracted from the impressions we were giving to the Soviet Bloc countries, and resulted in me being sent to Fort Campbell, Kentucky for a week serving as the drop-zone officer during test trials of the release mechanism.

One experience that did not turn out so well on that mission was one that occurred in the men's room just prior to our departure back to France. As you will learn on several occasions in this book, flying suits and I have a somewhat strained (or should I say stained?) relationship. Just prior to departure, I excused myself to use the men's room. As you will learn, flying suits require dropping trou all the way down to allow accomplishing number two. (For some of my prodigy, that means taking a crap).

This has nothing to do with me doing number two, but with some aircrew member doing number one before me. He couldn't have been a pilot, or if so, had partied too much the night before because his aim was terrible.

Rushing to the aircraft, with my flight suit soaked, I was not well received by fellow flight crew members, and resulting in me flying in my shorts and t-shirt while my flight suit swayed on the door at the very aft of the aircraft. You may feel this episode need not be included here, but the subject and my experiences with flight suits will be discussed in later chapters as well.

There were many funny things that occurred during my 18-month assignment to Sewart AFB, but I will recount just two more in the interest of keeping this chapter short, and probably preserving the dignity and reputation of some of my fellow squadron members.

We had a black loadmaster in the squadron whose first name was Shirley. His first name probably contributed to his becoming a Golden Glove boxer. Not on my flight, but another squadron crew, on a personnel parachute drop mission, Shirley was standing next to the open left parachute door, as was required by regulation. The loadmaster was also required to be wearing a parachute and interphone headset to be available to respond in the event of a hung trooper emergency. Apparently it had been a fairly rough flight weather-wise and several of the troopers felt called to use the "air sickness bags" (we called them something else).

One trooper felt called upon to show what he thought of the flight and the Air Force, by throwing the contents of his bag all over Shirley on his way out the paratroop door. Shirley took off his headset, unstrapped his security line, and jumped out behind the trooper. The trooper's chute opened immediately, allowing Shirley to free-fall below him keeping him in sight. When the trooper landed, he was met by Shirley who proceeded to pummel him severely. Shirley was completely exonerated when the matter was investigated. Now that's what I call military justice.

On the subject of airsickness bags, I would like to "bring up" another story. For the inauguration of President Kennedy, our wing was tasked with taking the Air Force Academy student corps to Washington, DC, to march in the inaugural parade. If you are old enough to remember, (and probably most of you are not) the country suffered from an extreme weather situation all across the nation. This resulted in Academy cadets being strung out all over the east coast area due to severe weather enroute and in Washington, DC. The enroute weather also resulted in turbulent flight conditions. The cadets were flying in their formal dress uniforms, and the aircrews had provided airsickness bags just in case. There was also a large garbage can located in the front of the cargo compartment. The seventy cadets per airplane were strapped in on the paratrooper configuration seats in the cargo compartment. Two enterprising cadets managed to position themselves at the front and the rear of one of the rows of seats. They had also arranged to covertly supply themselves with an airsickness bag containing chicken noodle soup. Midflight, the cadet at the rear of the aircraft pretended to use the barf bag (there I said it), rolled the top of it down and passed it forward gingerly from man to man to the front of the aircraft where his buddy opened it, looked inside it and proceeded to drink the chicken noodle soup. You can imagine the ensuing eruption throughout the cargo compartment. This story was confirmed to me recently by a USAFA graduate here in Boone who told me that he was on that very flight.

CHAPTER 5

Naha AB. Okinawa

The last chapter reminded me of my tour at Naha AB, Okinawa. Naha was my second permanent assignment after leaving pilot training. We were there from 1962 to 1965. I was still married to Carol Clodfelter. However, Okinawa and the Vietnam situation in the early sixties resulted in much more TDY travel and sitting alerts at Kadena AB (also located on Okinawa), in case of nuclear war. These influences, combined with typhoon evacuations and real party opportunities at the service clubs, created many more marital obstacles for couples.

For the most part Naha was quite an enjoyable assignment. I was upgraded to instructor pilot there, and flew many interesting missions as a member of E-flight, a highly classified unit that flew special missions. I was in the 21st TCS, one of three squadrons assigned to Naha. There had been only two when I arrived, but shortly after my arrival, my old squadron from Sewart AFB, was re-designated from the 62nd TCS to the 345th TCS and reassigned to Naha. Therefore, we had many old friends and families joining us.

Upon arrival, I built (using a local Okinawan contractor) a typical, small three bedroom house for $4000. When we moved onto base two years later, I sold it for $4000. I could have sold it for more, but I didn't want to rip off old friends coming over from Sewart AFB. I had three guys from the old squadron all wanting to buy it, so I sold it to the first one who had contacted me. After spending many years in real estate years later, I look back on that transaction as a real missed opportunity.

Most of our flights at Naha were for resupplying troops and supplies to Vietnam. We did have other missions however. We were all tactically qualified, and spent many hours flying close formation troop drops. I was made the project pilot for developing the HALO (High Altitude/Low Opening) drop program for the Special Forces (Green Berets), a new theory for dropping paratroopers from high altitudes letting them free fall to lower altitudes before opening their chutes and flying the chutes to distant landing sites. We developed the program on Ie Shima Island, the island where Ernie Pyle was killed in World War II.

We spent week-long TDY's to Kadena Air Base, (just up the road on Okinawa), where we sat on alert for a week at a time, with nine aircraft, each with nine nuclear bombs onboard, for evacuation during typhoons. Or, if the big balloon went up, we were to carry them to Korea and Japan, to be uploaded onto fighter/bombers, since the treaty with Japan wouldn't allow storing nuclear weapons on Japanese territory.

During one week, the squadron was sent to Clark Field in the Philippines for search and rescue. A contract carrier, Flying Tiger Airlines, lost an airliner transporting troops from the US to Vietnam. Our squadron spent several days searching at low altitude for survivors. We would shut down our outboard engines during the search to conserve fuel. This practice would not be allowed today. Our efforts were fruitless. No survivors were found.

During that mission, we had our airplanes at Clark, and a typhoon was approaching Okinawa where we were stationed and our families lived. Our crews were all put on one airplane to get us back to Okinawa. But this was not, as you might expect, to rescue our families, but to evacuate all of our remaining aircraft to Japan. These aircraft included those needing maintenance and real hanger queens, those aircraft constantly in need of maintenance and major repair. The winds were already too high for us to land at Naha, where our planes and our families were located. Because of already high crosswinds, they had to fly us into Kadena AB up the island. Our bus was police-escorted from Kadena to Naha, and upon arrival, we started the evacuation.

Being an instructor pilot does not necessarily mean having all of the advantages. They assigned all of us to the aircraft needing maintenance and the hanger queens, which would be the last to depart. Because of the high crosswinds, one of our pilots wiped out the threshold landing light system at the end of the runway, upon departure.

Our families gathered for the not unusual "typhoon parties" in different homes. They were accustomed to this exercise, as typhoons were not unusual in Okinawa.

We also had to evacuate the nuclear loaded birds from Kadena, when we were sitting alert and typhoons threatened. On one such occasion, I had to shut down an engine upon take off, which was usually no big deal in the overpowered A-model C-130, but a little scarier with nine nuclear weapons aboard. I proceeded on to Korea as assigned. That would probably not be allowed in today's Air Force, but things were different back then. (Those Were the Days!)

Speaking of typhoons. One time the alert came way too late for us to evacuate the airplanes, so we, as crews, started up all the planes sitting on the ramp and spent the night pivoting them in place, as the control tower would call out the wind direction changes. Talk about choreography!

As an E-flight pilot, I spent a lot of time on highly classified missions. Because one mission was declassified, I can mention it here. We were sent TDY to a highly classified base (at that time). It later became a fighter base named Takli. Our mission was to fly supplies to India, since the Chinese had invaded in the northern part of India. Even today, most folks don't know this happened. As it turned out, the Russians were also supporting India.

Since Burma was hostile to the US at the time, we had to circumnavigate it for fear of being shot down. This made for a long trip, since we could not remain overnight in Agra, India, due to the nature of our mission. However, we were given tours of the Taj Mahal and fed dinner while our aircraft was being unloaded and refueled. Some of us purchased souvenirs, which we were not allowed to show to our families.

Later, the Indian government presented a larger scale model of the Taj Mahal to our squadron as a gift of thanks. This blew the classification cover and we were allowed to show our small replicas of the Taj Mahal to our families (I still have mine to this day). That was in the early sixties, so I guess I could consider it an antique.

Before we started our flight back each night, they fed us Indian food for dinner. Although I still eat Indian food, I am quite wary about it. I will not explain why, but that flight was very long and cold without a flight suit. (I told you earlier about my experiences with flight suits.)

During the "Gulf of Tonkin" incident, (where the US greatly expanded involvement in South Vietnam), we were "hot bedding." We got what little sleep we could between our flights while our planes were being reloaded and refueled and we shared our cots in the hospital at Clark Field with incoming crews returning from Saigon. This is called "hot bedding". We were aroused when the next plane was ready to depart. We would then fly from Clark Field in the Philippines to Saigon, landing around the clock. The airbase in Saigon had no field lighting at night. We were prohibited from using landing lights except on very short final approaches. This included no taxi lights on the ground. We had to use wing walkers to preclude taxiing into other parked aircraft. Several fighter aircraft were lost crashing into mountains in the areas around the airfields.

The "hot bedding" was allowed due to the urgency of the mission, and higher headquarters waiving the mandatory crew rest required between duty-day limitations. Unfortunately, (or perhaps fortunately) the crew rest requirements were reinstated after one of our pilots taxied into an upright ramp fire extinguisher. The number one prop put a gash in the on/off faucet of the extinguisher, not really damaging the fire bottle. However, the small nick completely interrupted the prop rotation causing an off balance condition and separation of the prop from the engine. At full rotation speed when the prop hit the tarmac, it spun it into the number two engine, decoupling that prop, which smashed a large hole in the port fuselage. The accident investigation determined that crew fatigue had greatly influenced the incident that resulted in the reinstatement of mandatory crew rest and the end of "hot bedding."

The Naha assignment was quite enjoyable and eventful, not to mention the opportunities it presented to a practical-joker risk taker.

On one mission to Tachikawa AB in Japan, at the Officer's club, my crew and I ran into a flight nurse who had been dating a friend of mine in the 815th TCS. His name was Ken, last name omitted in order to protect the innocent, not because he was married, because he was a bachelor. I don't want him to take the blame for what follows.

My crew and I left the Officers club with the nurse with a stop off

The Captured Flying Jenny 1964 L to R: Reneau, Frankenberg, Keller and Squadron Commander Lt. Col Carlson (the Claw)

at her quarters to pick up a hacksaw. The 815th TCS was known as the "Flying Jennies"(for those urbanites, a Jennie is a female Jackass). They had a 4 ft. by 4 ft. tin Flying Jenny on top of a 20 ft. pole in front of their squadron building. We shinnied up the pole, hacksaw in hand, and managed to saw the pole, rescuing the Jenny. I think we had all three of us on the pole in order to hand the Jenny down. I might add here that Ken, the nurse's boyfriend, was the duty officer for the squadron. He remained asleep in the squadron, while the dirty deed was accomplished.

The nurse had a pilot friend with Air America, who agreed to fly the Jenny to Okinawa, where I had arranged to have it picked up by a fellow 21st TCS pilot at the passenger terminal. The next morning, as we were taxing out for takeoff we were instructed to hold in the run-up area. I had expected this, and thus pre-arranged the Air America transfer.

John Dale, a pilot in the 815th TCS (also a prankster) pulled up in front of my aircraft in a staff car in order to inspect our cargo. I readily agreed, but not without putting my inboard props slightly in reverse only to momentarily relieve John of his flight cap as he approached my aircraft. His search was obviously in vain, although he felt very strongly that it was I who had absconded with the tin ass.

The 815th squadron commander and crew went to Naha later, and as he was attending a weather briefing, he accidently fired a round from his service weapon, with the bullet lodging in the wall of the weather office. This gave us the perfect opportunity to pull another prank. We fired a bullet into the Flying Jenny's head, repainted her, and pinned a Purple Heart medal on her chest. We made fake medals with a donkey attached to a ribbon for me and my crew to wear on our formal mess dress uniforms at the 815th squadron's formal dress "Dining Out" banquet in Tachikawa. I wrote an appropriate soliloquy. We slipped into their formal dance wearing our medals and during a band's break, we made a formal return of the tin Jenny to the squadron.

I had written a poem to read to the gathered partiers. The poem's last line read "Shot a hole in your little red ass." By the way, I have the photos to back up this story. It is amazing what fun a little prank can generate. This action resulted in many months of paraphernalia thefts between the two squadrons.

Do you recall the incident at Wheelus Air Base requiring us to fly "inebriated?" A similar incident occurred on one of our highly classified missions. I was the aircraft commander, and though we were not inebriated, we had had a couple of beers after a long trip to and from Agra, India. We were relaxing at the make shift bar at a then-secret base.

There was a fighter squadron also stationed at the base. During our libations, the flight surgeon from that unit came running up with an emergency request. A local Thai baby had been determined to have a critical medical situation, and needed to be transported to Bangkok and was in desperate need of 100% oxygen en-route.

The flight surgeon had managed to commandeer a mobile oxygen replenishment cart and a standard suit hang-up bag. We didn't need the cart, as we could transfer the baby in the clothes hang-up bag onto our aircraft oxygen system. The flight surgeon accompanied us, but it was imperative we get to Bangkok as soon as possible.

Wearing tee shirts, shorts, and sandals, and having had a few beers, we cranked up and headed toward Bangkok. Without clearance, and unknown to air traffic control, since we were operating secretly in their country, I flew low-level, well-beneath-radar coverage so as not to disclose our operating location. Our support group had contacted the American detachment at Bangkok and they arranged to have a military ambulance and medical crew meet us on the ramp.

I popped up just before final approach, declaring visual flight rules, and a landing. It was granted. We were met on the ramp by a military ambulance and medics who took it from there.

I requested immediate take off under visual flight rules. The tower cleared me in a somewhat questioning voice. "Sir we are forecasting thunderstorms and we advise you depart Instrument Flight Rules." I answered, "Yes I know, I just came through them, and we have radar onboard." He was probably saying "these crazy Americans," but he cleared me for takeoff. I had to stay low on the return so as not to give away our secret base location from which we were operating a highly classified mission, since declassified. (Read Taj Mahal and flight suit). The flight surgeon stayed with the child, but had told me that because of the 100% oxygen, the baby would probably be blind if it survived, but he felt the risk was worth it.

Then there was the time a fellow pilot who was also in Saigon on a mission, warned me that I had better be prepared to do some "splaining" when I returned to Naha, as the wing commander was very upset that I had been blamed for smuggling civilians into Bangkok. He was correct, since the Officer of the Day, met my plane with orders to have me report immediately to the wing commander.

I had been in charge of organizing the 21st birthday party for the 21st Troop Carrier Squadron. It was a big bash to include the entire squadron buying blue blazers and grey flannel pants with embroidered squadron patches on the blazer pocket.

I had invited, with command approval, Ron Finney and his wife from Clark AB to join the celebration. Ron was the CALSU (Combined Airlift Support Unit) commander at Clark, and a squadron legend. He had managed to bring back a C-130 on a single engine. He and his crew had performed what we called "Elm tree maintenance," (wire and duct tape repairs) on three engines in order to get the aircraft out of a classified base in South Vietnam. We all had to do this at times, but to make a long story short, the maintenance was not adequate, and he lost the three engines in route home. The brass didn't know whether to court-martial him or give him a medal. They ended up giving him an "able aeronaut award." Had they court-martialed him, there would have been a lot of C-130s left stranded in Vietnam by career-protecting pilots.

I digress. Apparently, an aerial port airman had observed Ron and his wife Kathy, along with another married couple (who had only dropped them off at the aircraft), boarding my aircraft to be dropped off at Clark AB in route to Saigon. He checked and saw that they hadn't been processed through his passenger service unit.

We had used a procedure I had learned as a copilot when we were transiting through Tachikawa Air Base in Japan to Korea. It was Christmas time and a group of enlisted personnel was trying to get home to Korea to celebrate with their families.

They had been bumped from MAC (Military Air Command) passenger service because they hadn't arrived early enough to be properly manifested. Since we just popped in on short notice, they were left in the terminal. When we learned of their dilemma, we manifested them through the Pacific Air Force (PACAF) Arial port unit, and loaded them onto the aircraft.

Just prior to engine start, a MAC Second Lt. came aboard and ordered the passengers off the plane because they hadn't been manifested properly by MAC passenger service.

My wise old aircraft commander told me to take our flight plan, put a carbon under it, and list all the passengers as crew members, give a copy to the Second Lt. and usher him off the plane, a perfectly legal procedure.

This made for very happy enlisted travelers, as well as my Wing Commander, when I explained that was what had happened regarding smuggling civilians to Saigon. (Wow, this was a long episode.)

CHAPTER 6

The Eastern test range and the Gemini space program

Following our three year tour at Naha, a few of us were PCS'd (permanent change of station) to Patrick AFB, Florida, at Cape Kennedy to fly in support of the space programs and specifically the Gemini Space Program.

We flew telemetry and voice relay missions for each Gemini capsule recovery, or "splashdown," as we referred to them. During re-entry, the capsule generates a large heat buildup which creates a very limited range broadcast of telemetry and radio communications. (Telemetry is the transmission of vital biological information on the astronauts and mechanical conditions of the spacecraft.)

Voice relay is required in order for ground stations to communicate with the astronauts during the reentry phase, due to the limited range of the radios. Because of our "mission specific" position monitoring equipment, we also served as beacons for rescue aircraft and ships in the event of missed coordinate information for splashdown. I was actually on top of all the Gemini splashdowns except one capsule, which had to be brought down early, and landed in the Pacific Ocean instead of the proposed landing site, where NASA's entire recovery group was assembled.

When we weren't flying in direct support of the Gemini program, we were involved in regular range support. I was a designated STARS instructor pilot. STARS stands for Surface to Air Recovery System.

The Eastern Test Range maintains several down range ships for telemetry support of all the space shots, including orbital satellites. Their telemetry tapes needed to be returned to the Cape and Houston in a timely manner. Therefore, we would fly long distances (including into the Indian Ocean) to swoop down on these ships and snag large balloons tethered to data capsules on their decks. We would then winch them up into our aircraft using the All American Recovery System.

Our aircraft would extend a 20 ft. pole that contained two grappling hooks imbedded in its leading edge. We would fly just over the 18 ft.

long balloon, breaking it and snagging its rope harness with a grappling hook. The harness rope was a very expensive invention that allowed for a good bit of stretching. This would let the capsule slowly lift off the deck of the ship and allowed us to winch it up and aboard.

The capsule looked like an ocean buoy that you see marking shipping harbor

The Surface to Air Recovery System (STARS)

lanes. It stood about five feet tall with a three-foot diameter at its widest, narrowing to about 18-inch diameter at the top for aerodynamic stability. It closely resembled the actual Gemini space capsule except for size. Once aboard, we would fly it back to the Cape. The capsule also contained a good-sized storage area for administrative purposes, in addition to the storage area for the telemetry. It usually contained personal mail that ship crewmembers wanted us to mail once we got back to the States. The ship's cooks always insured there was some delicious food for our crew. Often these meals included fried chicken, steaks, and seafood. They always included cookies and desserts.

An interesting sidelight that I learned from several members of the ships' crews was that they had developed an elaborate gambling program for these STARS pickups. There weren't too many STARS qualified pilots in the unit but the ships' crews had the names of those of us who were. They would always ask us in route who the pilots were. We found out that they had handicapped each one of us as to how many passes it would take the pilot to make the grab. I was told by several ship crewmembers that I was the odds-on favorite to make the grab on the first pass. Apparently, that word made its way back to our operations officer. It was no surprise to him, as I was the STARS instructor, and had developed a method of throwing the hooks into the balloon line using the rudders on the possibility of a close miss. This becomes a tougher job in that the balloon always aligns itself facing into the wind, which creates a crosswind approach for us. My students were always leery of using this technique; as they weren't sure of the aircraft's capability in an extreme yaw situation (to yaw an aircraft you cross control the rudders and ailerons to swing the tail of the aircraft). I might add that this reputation gained for me a lot of long-range pick-up missions, as fuel could become a very important aspect of completing a successful mission. Sometimes we didn't have much time to waste on long range or questionable weather situations.

It was here at Patrick where I learned about my wife's infidelities, and I obtained a divorce. My lawyer maintained that as I was now a bachelor, the girls would be better off staying with their mother, and that I should supply child support, but not alimony. It was really tough and I missed my daughters very much, but I had continued contact with them. Subsequently,, they blended well into my new family and we are still very close.

After a year as a bachelor, I met Dottie Rutz, whom I mentioned at the beginning of this book. (Remember the blind date with the little white lie about my tennis enthusiasm?) We fell in love and were married. We had a wonderful life until cancer took her 43 years later. Dottie was an elementary school teacher when we met, and had taught in Maryland while living in Georgetown. She also returned to Washington to work as a boiler-room girl for Barry Goldwater's election campaign. She wrote speeches for him, apparently not good enough for a win, but did meet with him regularly and others for breakfast.

Let me tell you about my proposal. We had friends Rick and Trici Collins who sponsored our blind date. They had a sailboat and as we were dating, Dottie and I enjoyed sailing with them.

While we were just dating, we visited her parents in Ft. Lauderdale where I saw an ad in the paper for a Hurricane sailboat (an 18 ft. racing scow).

Patrick AFB, Florida, is located at the confluence of the Banana and Indian rivers. The confluence is part of the Inland Waterway System and becomes very wide at the point where the base is located. Therefore, it is an ideal location for sailing.

Co-owners of the sail boat,
"Dottie's Dimple"

We looked at the sailboat and I wanted to buy it, but I didn't have my checkbook with me. This beautiful young teacher offered to write a check to cover it as a loan. I was driving my 1965 Mustang fastback with a trailer hitch, so I took her up on the offer.

As we were pulling the sailboat back to Patrick AFB, she asked that since she had loaned me the money for it, "could she be the first mate on it?"

Without hesitation, I answered, "No."

She asked, "Why?"

I answered that I would pay her back as I didn't want to be beholden to anyone. But, I wisely added "You can't be the first mate, but I would like you to be "half owner as my wife." What could the poor girl do? Here she was a hundred miles from home with a bold risk-taking Air Force Pilot who owed her money. With coercion like that in the works, she gave me that 'just-you-wait' grin I mentioned earlier and answered, "Of course." I guess you could say I got hooked in a couple of ways: smart lady and I was a really smart risk-taker.

I don't travel anywhere now without my checkbook, but look what I would have missed out on had I had it with me then.

We had a great year of sailing, (our military housing was right on the river), and sports car rallying, (she owned a 1964 Porsche). We sold the sailboat with a sign reading "FOR SAIL, CAPTAIN, GOIN' TO S.E.A." (S.E.A. is also an acronym for South East Asia).

After my S.E.A. tour, we took the Porsche to Germany for our four years there, and took it everywhere else until 2009, when we finally decided to sell it for more than she paid for it new in 1964.

CHAPTER 7

Visiting my Mom and Dad

Following three years at Patrick AFB, where this autobiography began, I received PCS orders to UBON Royal Thai Air Base in Thailand, and I was on my way.

After waiting out a big snowstorm in the Albuquerque airport, we finally arrived (in a blinding snowstorm) at Farmington, New Mexico municipal airport (one small terminal building). We stopped there to visit my mom and dad, and drop off our son Rob while Dottie and I proceeded to Las Vegas, Nevada, and finally to Travis AFB, where I would be departing for Vietnam. Mom and Dad couldn't have been more pleased to be left with our nearly one-year-old future risk-taker.

Mom and Dad were also risk-takers. They met in Boston, Massachusetts, where he was a divinity school student from Oklahoma at Boston University. She was from Northampton, Massachusetts, and a graduate from Smith College. She was employed as a social worker.

Looking at dad's photo albums, he had quite a few girlfriends while in Boston, but really fell for "Shorty" as he called her.

Mom was only 5 feet tall and Dad was still calling her that even after I grew up (if in fact I ever did grow up). One of the interesting stories Dad tells about their courtship, and one of the reasons he really fell for her, dated from an event while he was the athletic director at camp Waldron, a church camp for disadvantaged boys from the Boston area.

During the time he was away at camp, he grew a mustache. When Mom came up to see him on a weekend, she didn't like it and asked him to shave it off. Maybe I got a little of my mischievousness from Dad, because when he spied a wheelbarrow filled with bricks, he told Mom that if she could push that brick-filled wheelbarrow up a nearby steep hill, he would shave it off. Before she left that afternoon for Boston, Dad was clean-shaven again. There was no stopping "Shorty" when she set her mind to it. I experienced that on many occasions as I was growing up.

Mom's big risk-taking experience as a Smith graduate was marrying a poor Oklahoma preacher and driving back with him from Massachusetts to Oklahoma in a dilapidated old car they named "Geronimo." They later sold the car for seven dollars and fifty cents. Along with their marriage license came the Depression and the Dust Bowl.

Dad and Mom Reneau

To add to their risk taking, when I was three years old and Jack, my brother, was a newborn, Dad volunteered to join the army as a chaplain. He had his landing craft blown out from under him as he went ashore (unarmed), onto Omaha Beach during the Allies' invasion of Normandy.

He participated in the Battle of the Bulge and many other campaigns and remained there throughout the war. Meanwhile, "Shorty" was raising two mischievous risk-takers by herself while serving as PTA president and Sunday School Superintendent at first Methodist Church in Lawton, OK.

At 6 years old, I would hitchhike out to Ft. Sill to play on the army's obstacle course. I poked a hole in my head while attempting to swing from a railroad trestle using doubled up hay-bailing cord, and rode my bicycle to a football game by myself and someone backed over it with their car, resulting in my pushing it several miles home with a warped wheel. (There will be more on Mom & Dad throughout this narrative.)

CHAPTER 8

The Risk-taker hits Las Vegas and points west

Our trip to Las Vegas was uneventful except that my risk-taking at blackjack turned out like my trestle-swinging and football-game-attendance.

One of the highlights of Las Vegas was that the Bradleys, dear friends from Patrick AFB., entertained us. Diana Bradley worked for an entertainment magazine and we were given free front row tickets to all the big casino shows.

I departed Travis AFB on my way to Thailand and eventually Vietnam, but not without a stop at "Snake School." Snake School was the name everyone gave to the mandatory jungle survival course at Clark AB in the Philippines. The school was looked upon as a blessing and an experience filled with terror. I had already attended the escape and evasion survival school at Stead AFB in Reno, Nevada, just after finishing pilot training.

Survival schools in general are not very pleasant. I have attended three survival schools including a water survival school where they dragged the participant behind a boat face down and dropped them from a parasail leaving the man adrift in a one man raft for several hours on Biscayne Bay. I previously attended the dreaded escape and evasion school after pilot training where one had to survive in the wild and run an escape course. If captured, and even if not captured, the soldier was put in a highly stressful POW camp manned by truly sadistic enemy-portraying guards. This included some torture, cramped confinement, and interrogation techniques.

I made it through the escape course, which I attributed to my excellent conditioning as a college athlete. In fact, I returned to my Quonset hut (meager sleeping quarters) fully expecting to be chased down and returned to the POW camp. I was not disappointed, because that's exactly what happened.

After the POW experiences, we were taken up into the mountains for survival training for several days.

As fortune would have it, after several days of surviving, a large forest fire broke out between California and Reno. We were forced to be firefighters; because of that, they had to feed us. This ruined the starvation and escape and evasion portion of the training.

At night, we slept around large controlled open fires, burning up on one side of our bodies and freezing on the other side.

A firefighting plane crashed near us and we watched as they brought the pilot's body out on a bulldozer. I remembered that scene many years later as we were preparing to go into combat.

Eventually the fire got away from the firefighters and burned the main power system providing electricity to Reno and Stead AFB. They evacuated us, returned us to Stead, and sent us on our way with no dinners or hot showers. We all felt cheated, as it was customary to celebrate graduating survival school students with a big dinner party at government expense at the Sparks Casino.

In comparison to the Stead survival school years earlier, jungle school was a blessing, as we knew that we were going into combat, and there was a real chance that we would really need the training.

In fact, they told us that the shortest time between completion of the course and being shot down was just a matter of a few hours. One fighter pilot's squadron was short of pilots and sent an F-4 with an empty back seat to pick him up at Clark AB. Enroute to their base in Thailand, they were shot down.

Once again, I was blessed while I was at jungle survival school, in that mountain landslides in the Philippines caused the night escape and evasion/navigation portion to be cancelled. So they took us back to Clark AB and sent us on our way partially trained, into who knows what.

Except for the jungle school, Clark AB was a great place to be. I had been there many times when I was stationed at Naha Air Base on Okinawa.

CHAPTER 9

1968-1969: "Death from Above"

My next stop was Bangkok, then on to join (or I should say start up) the 14thAir Commando Unit, at Ubon Royal Thai AB. We were the prototype AC-130 gunship squadron. Several months later, we were re-designated as the 16th Special Operations Squadron under the 8th Tactical Fighter Wing. We were a motley crew with only one aircraft. We had six pilots including the squadron commander and operations officer, and six navigators. We also had our enlisted flight crewmembers, gunners, and maintenance personnel.

Although I was the junior pilot (by a couple of weeks), I had the most C-130 flying hours, and therefore was designated one of the two instructor pilots, the squadron maintenance officer, and chief of the gunners' section. All the officers had additional duty responsibilities.

Wearing three hats was fairly easy, since we primarily flew at night, giving us time during the day (after post-mission partying and crew rest) to accomplish our additional duties. Given the fact that we flew almost every night, we kept busy and the year passed by relatively quickly.

Colonel Robin Olds had been the Wing Commander and had decreed that, "Since my crews fly all night, all the support facilities will operate on a twenty-four hour basis as well." This included all support offices, the swimming pools, the movie theatre, the barbershop, and, of course, the clubs. Sometimes that meant that we could be found partying at the O-Club bar on an early Sunday morning, while other base personnel were on their way through the club to church.

Of course, there was the daily awareness that, depending on the accuracy of the enemy gunners, we could be ending our tour early by going home to our maker, or take up rent-free tenancy in the Hanoi Hilton or some other God-forsaken POW situation. There was also the possibility of ending up in a survival situation, or in a bamboo "Tiger Cage," a term used for a jungle prisoner abode.

Sometimes these thoughts could make crew members think not so critically about those of our contemporaries who chose to spend the duration of the war in Canada. Fortunately, for them, President Jimmy Carter made it easy for them to return. I now live in a university town and run into some of them who are now retired. (I think I had best let that subject die, because I might need some scholarly help on getting this autobiography printed.)

This chapter will probably be the most interesting one for most of you, especially those up-and-coming risk-taking younger members of my prodigy. I have decided to go into these experiences here, instead of including an unedited appendix in the form of the long letter I had referred to in the introduction.

In 1967, Ron Terry, the developer of the gunship concept, and a few TDY crewmembers brought the prototype AC-130 to Southeast Asia for testing. They operated primarily out of Nha Trang, South Vietnam. They were not in country too long, but long enough to prove how valuable a weapons system they had in the AC-130. They returned to the States to iron out some of the wrinkles and further sell the project. They returned in early 1968 to Ubon RTAB in a TDY status to train the initial cadre of PCS troops; that was us.

Our initial designation was Det. 2, 14th Air Commando Group. We had six pilots, six navigators, two flight engineers, and an illuminator operator. We also had a few gunners and a cadre of several maintenance folks.

Our six pilots were Lt Col Garvey Fink, (Detachment Commander), Lt Col Charlie Koeninger, (Operations Officer), Majors Paul Zook and Bill Olsen, and Captains Tom Sparr and Bob Reneau. Our navigators were Lt.Col. Al Cross, Captains Thurston (Corky) Yoshina, Hal Welsh, Tom George, Cal Taylor and Bill Tunicliff. I wish I could remember the names of all of our enlisted crewmembers and maintenance personnel, but to name those I do remember would do a disservice to those fantastic guys whose names have slipped my mind.

This small cadre ran the program from early 1968 until the follow-on birds and replacement troops started arriving from Lockbourne AFB in late 1968. Most historical documentation forgets about us as we were somewhat bastard sons, being 14th Air Commander Troops on the 8th Tactical Fighter Wing base for a goodly portion of our tour, and the fact that we operated out of Tan Son Nhut AB in Saigon for a considerable time while the monsoon season was in full swing in Laos.

We had only one gunship, and we flew it every night. Sometimes we would fly several missions a night, switching seats, and therefore, call signs. We used our individual call signs to try to convince the enemy that we had more than one aircraft.

The individual call signs are another interesting story. We not

Some initial cadre crew members

only used them to hopefully confuse enemy intelligence, but we thought it would be an interesting way to preserve for historical and reunion purposes…a continuing list of gunship pilots…since due to experience qualifications, every pilot was qualified to be pilot in command. That changed after we left, and the squadron eventually grew into the largest squadron in the Air Force. We reserved the call sign Spectre 01 for the acting squadron commander to use when he was actually flying missions, but had a chronologically assigned permanent call sign. Therefore, being the most junior pilot, but also the sixth most senior pilot, I was Spectre 07, hence the title of this autobiography.

As I mentioned earlier, I was put in charge of the gunners, a small group of weapons specialists whose duty was to clear firing jams, shovel spent and unspent ammo brass, and serve as anti-aircraft artillery observers, sitting in the open escape hatch on the right (blind) side of the aircraft.

Let me elaborate on the shoveling brass aspect I mentioned. The four 20 millimeter Vulcan cannons we had and the four 7.62 millimeter Gatling guns were each capable of firing 3000 rounds per minute. We had the Vulcans choked down to fifteen hundred rounds per minute. We usually only fired in one second bursts in order to keep from melting down the barrels of the cannon. This would give us twenty-five rounds per firing per gun. Each round of the high explosive incendiary (HEI) was the equivalent of a hand grenade, exploding when it hit, therefore increasing its kill ratio proportionately. (It also lessened the need for complete firing accuracy). The mechanical problem this procedure presented was that at the end of each burst, the gun would spit out six rounds of live ammunition along with the spent cartridges. Since the gunship was meant to operate around and amid troops in conflict, we could not jettison our spent cartridges and metal belt clips below us for fear of collateral damage to troops and civilians on the ground. Therefore, we had to jettison it into large metal bins. The gunners then had to shovel it all into canvas bags, with metal shovels, live rounds and all, with the live rounds being recycled.

Interestingly enough, this presented a problem of which we were unaware until several months into the mission. We had been flying nonchalantly around and through lines of thunderstorms on our missions. One day a tech representative from the Vulcan cannon company stopped in to observe our operations. When he discovered the metal brass bins and metal shovels, he put on a demonstration for us. He got hold of an old cloth automobile seat and placed it behind one of the unloaded Vulcan cannons. He proceeded to slide his bottom across the cloth seat and touched the electrical firing mechanism of the cannon. That small amount of electricity generated by the seat of his pants caused the unloaded chamber of the gun to rotate and consequently fire (if it were loaded). Since we carried thousands of rounds of electrically fired ammunition, you can only imagine what a bolt of lightning would cause.

One thing this demonstration caused was altering our thoughts about operating in thunderstorm areas. We also immediately switched to plastic shovels for the gunners shoveling live rounds in the metal brass reclamation bins.

Another gun incident occurred when one of the Vulcan cannons cooked off (started firing) while the aircraft was parked in the revetment (sand bagged and armored aircraft parking space) at Ubon. Fortunately, the shells lodged in the sandbagged revetment wall and didn't explode because the projectile hadn't revolved the minimum number of revolutions to arm the explosive charge before imbedding in the sand bags.

I have often stated that although we were flying the state of the art weapons system at the time, compared to the later versions it was like driving a Model-A Ford compared to today's Mercedes. The early birds were A-models with the three-bladed Aero-Products propeller. In addition, the hydraulic pressure boost system to the rudder was not reduced, giving more and stronger rudder response. These features combined with the lower gross weight (124,000 lbs.), gave us much more maneuverability than the follow-on birds. I could put in full left rudder, virtually turn on a dime, and completely change my firing orbit geometry. I picked up the nickname "Rudders Reneau" from a few of the guys in the back who suffered through the maneuver because of its somewhat violent characteristic. My philosophy was that better the maneuver than being shot down by upcoming Triple AAA (anti-aircraft artillery). I remember on a couple of occasions, it allowed me to knock out two 37mm AAA sites that were firing at us from places separated by considerable distance. I was firing on the first AAA site, which was in our normal nine o'clock position. The second AAA site fired at us from the seven o'clock position, relative to our firing position. He was apparently figuring that it would take us another orbit to pick him up. Obviously, he didn't have another think coming…or any other thought, for that matter.

Although we had a very rudimentary fire-control computer, which was supposedly able to consider the winds, we didn't use it because of its unreliability.

We had four 20-millimeter Vulcan cannons and four 7.62-millimeter Mini guns. These were fixed and untrainable, requiring aircraft repositioning for aiming and firing purposes. On many occasions, this necessitated the fire, adjust, and fire again technique by the pilot, who did all the aiming and firing. We had several different types of acquisition sensors which were good for getting us into firing position, but didn't take wind into consideration. We had to rely on our flight controls to maintain our firing geometry.

Since the pilot did all the firing and correcting, our effectiveness was highly dependent on our being in the correct geometry. Our airspeed had to be exactly 150 Knots. The co-pilot controlled this. Our angle of bank had to be 30 degrees and was called out continuously by the flight engineer during the firing phase. Our altitude had to be exact and we left this up to the autopilot. We did not fly without the autopilot. I remember several occasions, where I, as the maintenance officer, used our priority to cannibalize autopilots from other C-130s.

We flew with two pilots: pilot and co-pilot; sometimes three. The third pilot was usually a trainee, instructor, or observer. We had four navigators, a flight engineer, four gunners, and an illuminator operator. In the early days, we had an officer from Sandia Labs working on a special project using a device to determine the counter actions capability of the enemy. His equipment was integrated into the aiming computer system in order that we could fire on targets he was able to detect.

The four navigators were the table navigator, the night optical device (NOD) operator, the Infrared (IR) detector operator, and the TV operator.

The Illuminator operator served as an aft scanner, flares launcher, and ran the 20-KVA searchlight that we could operate out the back of the aircraft in either the overt or the infrared mode. We flew with the aft ramp and door open, in order to be able to jettison the flare launcher in the event AAA hit it. It contained many highly volatile phosphorous flares. We also needed the ramp open to enable us to move the illuminator searchlight out the back so it could be directed electronically to provide battle field lighting in the overt mode and/or infrared mode where only soldiers wearing night visual goggles could see the enemy.

A typical mission would begin with dinner at the club (or mess hall), a short trip to the flight line to don our survival gear, obtain the weather report, and check on the latest intelligence information, AAA locations, and truck traffic information, this usually having been supplied by us from our mission the previous night. We would also sanitize ourselves. (That doesn't mean we took a shower.) "Sanitizing" means that we had to ensure we weren't wearing or carrying anything that would reveal to the enemy anything regarding the mission, the aircraft, or organization. Rank was OK, as it was required by the Geneva Convention to be revealed, if captured.

An interesting side note to this is that in the early days, we didn't fly in flight suits. (Here we go again with flight suits.) I don't know how long this procedure lasted after our departure, but here is our rational: In the prototype bird, we didn't have an electronically operated NOD (night optical device) seat, and the NOD operator spent the mission doing deep knee bends in attempting to acquire targets. His position was in the open air space of the removed crew entrance door, exposing himself to AAA and small arms. If we had extra crewmembers, they would spell the NOD operator. That position required wearing a flack vest, flack helmet, and parachute, along with a survival vest that included radios, a 45 caliber pistol with extra ammunition belts, an extra battery for radio, signaling items, blood chits (classified survival packet), etc. If we wore flight suits that had many pockets filled with whatever, the entire weight was borne by the shoulders.

We wore long sleeved fatigues which had many advantages, some obvious and some not so obvious.

Fatigues had a belt, useful in many respects, among them survival, first aid, cooling, providing ventilation or (shirt removal) instead of dropping the flight suit around the waist. This also aided in dropping one's pants without detection to allow for biological necessities. The fatigues also had drawstrings around the ankles to discourage bug infestation in a jungle survival situation.

Our survival vests could be very heavy with just the minimum requirements. Some of our replacement crewmembers chose to load up any extra vest pocket space with extra pistol ammunition. We, being logical thinkers, put in extra survival radio batteries, planning to use our pistols to kill threatening animals as opposed to further antagonizing large groups of the enemy in a last ditch "Custer's Last Stand" operation.

After the personal preparation phase, we would proceed to the airplane and accomplish our pre-takeoff procedures, which included a "ceremonial piss" as some would claim. I always thought of it as a nervous piss, just as for the reason all racing swimmers dive into the pool prior to the start. (I advise beginning young racing swimmers not to ingest pool water near the start of a race.) I digress.

After takeoff, we would circle a highly visible landmark on the ground to align our sensors and guns. In Ubon, it was the fountain in the center of town. In Saigon, it was the lighted tetrahedral (wind direction indicator) in the runway infield at Tan Son Nhut Air Base.

An interesting and somewhat scary situation occurred one night flying out of Ubon. After crossing the fence, (entering Laos) the engineer armed one of the Vulcan cannons and, as I made a radio call to Moonbeam (one of our monitoring/directing air borne aircraft), the gun fired. "Whoa," that's not supposed to happen. We returned to base to discover that because the trigger is located just below the pilot's radio transmit switch, a repair to the radio switch the afternoon prior to that night's mission had resulted in some solder dripping down and making a connection between the two.

Now is where the scary thought comes in. Had I made a radio transmission, and an arming switch been on during the sensor alignment process, the main center and all the citizens of Ubon and many Americans gathered around would have been blown to bits.

Now we can get back to the mission and crossing the fence. Crossing the fence is a critical time as we were crossing into hostile territory. At this time, all lights inside and outside the aircraft were turned off. All cigarettes were extinguished. The curtain around the table navigator, who needed table lighting, was tightly drawn and secured.

In the early days, we had pretty much a free reign on our operations. We operated independently from the 8th TFW. We flew where we wanted in terms of looking for targets, as opposed to being fragged (assigned) to specific areas by higher command and control, as was the case when we returned from Saigon. During our months in Saigon, due to the monsoon season affecting our mission on the Ho Chi Minh trails,

President Lyndon Johnson declared a moratorium on the operations in Laos that allowed the enemy to move a lot of heavy AAA into Laos, making it much tougher for us to operate.

In the beginning, we could be pretty casual about our orbits and length of time in each orbit. Our procedure originally had us paralleling the roads. This, however, resulted in surprise AAA coming up from directly below us. We changed our tactics to an approach perpendicular to the roads, making quick scans down or up the roads as we crossed. If we found trucks, we would engage immediately or mark their position. Sometimes we would drop a log flare, a non-parachute flare that burns at extreme temperatures on the ground lasting for 30 minutes and could not be extinguished by ground personnel. It would ignite on the way down and give us a good reference point for coming back later from a better acquisition course so we could acquire the target, fire, destroy, and get on our way before the AAA knew we were there.

We had a funny thing happen one night with a log flare. We threw one out to mark a couple of trucks. Returning to reap our reward of a kill, the NOD operator said, "you are not going to believe this, but the flare is not stationary." Shortly thereafter, we congratulated the IO (illuminator operator) for a perfect IP (impact point) hit. The flare had landed in the back of one of the trucks, and the driver was high tailing it down the trail as fast as he could. I thought that somewhat curious, because if I had one of those things burning in the middle of my cargo, I would have abandoned the truck, cargo, and everything, fearing an explosion. It wasn't long before that happened, and the truck blew up. We gave the IO credit for a truck destroyed. My curiosity as to why he was in such a hurry to drive away with that flare in the back, led me to think the driver had made a conscious decision to leave the area. We returned to the original position. I fired some rounds around the position where we had originally acquired the trucks. Lo and behold, the whole world lit up. We had never seen such explosions. We even put our F-4 escorts in on it before they ran out of fuel. Apparently, we had happened upon a combination fuel and ammunition storage area. It was probably our single most effective mission over the trails.

Now is a good time to talk about AAA. The enemy had many types of AAA, some of it with tracers and some without. "Tracers" means that each round or random rounds in a stream were lit in order that the gunners could follow where they were shooting and adjust. They had

small stuff, (50 Caliber) medium stuff ZPU (a Russian/Chinese AAA weapon) that didn't have tracers, but came up in rounds of 50 and discharged upon reaching their maximum altitude, looking like popcorn popping, 23mm multi-round guns with tracers, and larger 37mm AAA, firing all tracers coming at us in streams of 5 projectiles. The 23 and 37 mm rounds carried explosive heads that would blow up if they hit something. They would also self-detonate upon reaching their maximum altitude of 17 thousand feet. Hooray, they missed us, but wait! When they self-

Close Call: AAA crease just below my pilot's seat and visible between my right shoulder and the pilot's lower window

detonate, all that shrapnel would fall to earth, and we were flying beneath it. "Such a life."

The 37's were the most prolifically located: around cities, along the trail, at crossroads, near ammo dumps, and even on top of the Karsts, the mountain ridges and cliffs all along the trail.

In addition to the above mentioned, we had the real heavy stuff thrown up at us, the radar-directed 57mm's and 85mm's and the dreaded SAMs (surface to air missiles), which we avoided at all costs. Fortunately, for us, the shoulder-fired SAMs came into the country towards the end of our tour. You might say we had a Fourth of July display every night.

We were fortunate to learn our trade in combat, rather than at Lockbourne AFB in the States, where all follow-on crews were trained.

Because we operated with slowly increasing AAA, we quite easily adjusted to the escalating AAA environment. Since we were a new weapons system, the enemy also had to learn to defend against us as time ensued.

Now is a good time to tell you about the trails. I have always felt that some North Vietnamese could write an extremely interesting book about the trail. When most people think about the Ho Chi Minh trail, they envision a jungle path with "coolie" type laborers carrying packs on their backs. There, of course, was that means of transport, but there were also real thoroughfares with eighteen-wheelers speeding along. There were good-sized highways that would disappear at the side of a good-sized river, only to start up again on the other side (underwater bridges)! There were country roads that were blasted off the side of a mountain one night, only to appear the next night in perfect condition.

There was a persistent rumor passed around that the enemy was chaining American prisoners into the trucks we were destroying. I chose not to believe these rumors, considering them as propaganda. I had decided in my own mind that if that were the case, and I was in their situation (which could have been the case on any given night), I would have wanted the gunship to attempt to destroy the truck before it reached the Viet Cong, and the cargo be used to kill American soldiers. Obviously, that is an easy rationalization to make sitting safely back in the States, but it did help ease my conscience each time I pushed the trigger.

I have often thought looking back, that this tactic might have actually been the case, and partly accounted for the many MIAs (Missing In Action), as that action would have definitely been against the Geneva Convention. Admitting to this tactic would have resulted in world denunciation.

Before I describe a typical mission, I want to give you some information on my total assignment experience at Ubon. When we started out, our operations, command section, personal equipment section, maintenance, and gun maintenance were all located in two small sheet metal hangers adjacent to the revetment where we parked our one aircraft. When we came under the 8th TFW we were moved to quarters, both for our operations and our billeting. We old troops stayed in the old hootches (sleeping quarters). After all, they were a little closer to the

Officers club. While on the subject of quarters, shortly after my arrival there came a knock on the door. It was our new roommate. Bill Olsen and I had only two of us assigned to our good-sized room. Some thoughtful housing officer surprised us with our new roommate. It was Jack, my brother. We had both signed paperwork waiving the Sullivan Brothers Act, by which, unless waived by us, the government could not assign sole siblings into combat at the same time. Jack was an F-4 maintenance officer. I knew he was going to Southeast Asia, but in the same room? Actually, I was grateful, as we were able to become closer and bond in this perilous assignment.

All of the modern ways of communications to home, that is Facetime, Facebook, Skype, and telephone (the first three were not even invented) and even the traditional telephone, were not available. Dottie and I each had purchased small cassette tape recorders, and kept the post office busy by sending one-hour tapes every day. Fortunately, I could mail them postage free from a combat zone.

You might think that with our flying all night, working our additional duties during the day and trying to get a little crew rest, and making one hour tapes, we would have little time for partying. Somehow, priorities being what they were, we had no problem with that. It sometimes got a little embarrassing to be right in the middle of partying when the rest of the wing was on their way to church. We did have the advantage of having the entire base facilities open 24 hours a day.

Robin Olds and Chappie James (you might want to look them up as "Blackman and Robin") had just departed when we arrived, but their influence was still felt, especially in the lifestyle that was exhibited at the clubs. You can imagine the mental processing of young pilots who were never sure if they would be returning after their next flight.

Two other clubs are worth mentioning. One was the downtown "Spectre" club that our airmen established. They rented a large residence and put in a bar, pool table, comfortable seating or lounging furniture, and had three or four bedrooms upstairs for poker, other games of chance, or in the event that some squadron member needed to spend the night instead of returning inebriated to the base, by either walking or on the Thai baht bus (a local city bus line that charged the equivalent of five cents to ride).

As officers, we were invited to participate in the club if we wished, and they even gave us club cards with our tactical call signs as club numbers. I did go to the club on occasion, but never remained overnight.

The other club was a private Officers club called the Night Owls Roost. The 497th tactical fighter squadron was nicknamed the "Night Owls." It was those F4 pilots who flew cover for us after the AAA got so heavy on the trail. They were armed with cluster bombs, and as we were qualified forward air controllers, we would put them in on lucrative targets when they were about to "Go Bingo" (run out of fuel). Their Battle Damage Assessment (BDA) grew so high that other fighter squadrons got jealous, causing higher command to start sharing the flying cover missions with those fighter squadrons not necessarily night fighters, nor even stationed at Ubon. This worked to the detriment of the mission, in that we could pre-brief and post-brief with the Night Owls, and discuss strategy – that is, how we would put them on targets without endangering the flight environment that could get crowded at times with AAA and other aircraft.

The point of this story appearing in the clubs section was that we never had to pay for drinks at their bar. They greatly admired us, but thought we were crazy to fly the way we did. It is interesting to note that although we constantly offered, and it was legal, we could never get any of them to fly with us on a mission.

There was an Air Force policy in place that would not allow general officers to fly on combat missions if not fully qualified and part of the mission. Since all general officers felt they could waive the policy, we developed a plan to satisfy their desires and egos.

When the follow-on troops arrived, they had to unlearn some of the things they had learned at Lockbourne from non-combat instructor pilots.

We did have the benefit of choosing our working areas so that we could gradually increase the levels of threat to the new pilots. We started them off in the least defended section of Laos called "Golf" or, as we referred to it, "The Monkey Farm." We took the adventure-seeking generals into this area. As an instructor pilot, I could let them fly in the left seat and actually fire the guns. Not being proficient, the general officers killed an awful lot of monkeys, thus the nickname "Monkey Farm." We would let them get their jollies off and then take them back to Ubon where they could go to the bar and brag about their "combat" mission. We would then rearm, refuel, and go to the real combat areas. Many people thought we were crazy to fly where and how we did, but we were not crazy enough to fly into 300 to 500 rounds of AAA with an unqualified fifty-year-old egomaniac in the left seat, or explain our actions to a flying safety board in the event of a tragedy. The same held true to a degree with the new follow-on troops in that we only took them into the heavy stuff when we felt they were really ready, and then, usually with them in the right seat as co-pilot.

Two field grade officers insisted that the best defensive measure against AAA was to break right out of geometry. Any gunship pilot worth his salt knows that breaking right keeps you in the known target position longer, points your guns to the moon, and carries you over unknown threat areas in a highly vulnerable position, where the pilot controlling the airplane cannot see and react. It does place the co-pilot between you and any AAA burst headed your way. This gives little comfort to co-pilots.

Paul Zook and I, (the two original instructor-pilots) went to the Ops Officer to beg him not to place one of those particular Lt. Cols. into the instructor position he was seeking after we left for the US. We firmly believed that, as he frequently declared at the bar; his goal was to win a Medal of Honor, or some other heroic award. He refused to listen to his instructors, as he had learned it all at Lockbourne. Our pleading fell on deaf ears. He was allowed to continue in his unenlightened ways. After we left, he lost an airplane to AAA, and a good friend of mine died in the crash landing. That friend had been one of our flight engineers at Patrick AFB.

I might add here, we did win one philosophical dispute with the new cadre. They wanted to establish a "top gun" competition, with recognition and fame going to the pilot with the most truck kills. We (the old timers) felt that could only lead to two things happening, both of them bad. They were starting to fly as assigned hard crews, and we felt that in such competition, especially in light of their relative inexperience, the temptation to pad BDA (Battle Damage Assessments) might arise. Even worse, in an attempt to gain recognition by some glory-hungry aircraft commander, unnecessary risks might be undertaken, and lives put at risk that need not have been. Fortunately, the big wigs listened to us.

A lot of the following tactics discussion comes from the letter I sent to the young man whose father was a Spectre crewmember, and who was seeking information for a book that I assume never was published. I am including it here in an attempt to make it more interesting for my younger progeny.

There are some real tricks to flying in high AAA areas. I will mention a few, but I will caveat these remarks by saying that these tactics were against conventional weapons (not heat seekers), or other guided weapons. In addition, some weapons do not use tracer ammunition. We had that kind also, and I feared it the most. Fortunately, most of the big stuff had tracers. The 55s and 85s were single shot, but they had the tracer characteristic, and the movement concept of avoidance applied to them.

As I mentioned before, we were very fortunate that when we were developing our skills on the trails, we were a new weapons system that the enemy had not faced before. Therefore, things started out at a low level of threat to us as they were adjusting to defending against our tactics. As the war went on, more and more AAA batteries were moved into Laos, and the traffic level on the trails increased considerably. All of this allowed us to grow up and improve as the situation changed and learn the tricks of the trade.

Here are some of "Reneau's helpful hints on surviving in high threat areas. First, if there is a full moon and a thin overcast above, think about returning to the club, or at least avoiding the high AAA areas. Or maybe go work the "Monkey Farm."

No matter how much they are throwing up at you, as long as the projectiles have movement in their appearance, they are not going to hit you. The less motion, the closer they will come. If you just see a light that is getting brighter or a stream of them, you had better bust your ass to change something. The easiest tactic is to increase your bank. However, you best be sure that this maneuver doesn't cause other upcoming tracers to cease their movement.

If you have acquired a "mover," target truck, and have expended a few rounds on it with no results, you had better pull off, or at least straighten out for a time. The same goes for a target that you have hit and you can't understand why he doesn't blow up. Never follow him trying to kill him. He is a decoy leading you into a "Flack Trap" where you will experience many AAA batteries firing at you at one time. If you do experience this living hell, be sure you have brought an extra flight suit that you can change into before landing. (See previously mentioned episodes involving flight suits.)

Do not allow smoking on the aircraft during combat missions. The bad guys have night sensors too, usually retrieved from one of our crashed FAC (forward aircraft controller/observer planes); we know from tests we were doing to try to determine how many they possessed. (I mentioned our additional crewmember from Sandia Labs earlier.) We found it inevitable that whenever a crewmember lit a cigarette, AAA was soon to follow.

Teach all your crewmembers these tactics and it is amazing how much more successful your mission will be. A panicky intercom call from an illuminator operator or side observer means a lot more to you if you know he knows how to read AAA.

I don't know why I included this section as I doubt any of you will ever be flying the gunship in combat. However, since you are still reading, I will tell you a story relating to the last comment.

You have to know your crewmembers, their voices, and their personalities. We had a crusty old gunner named Yarborough, who spoke with a real Southern drawl. One night when I was on target, his voice came over the intercom, "Captain, we got thirty-seven coming up from our four o'clock. It looks like it might be close." "Captain, I think it's gonna hit us …, Gawd Damn, I bet you a case of beer it's gonna blow us out of the f…..g…" (By this time, knowing how much a case of beer meant to Yarborough, I was rolling left as hard as possible). Usually you could tell by the volume, pitch, and speed of the crewmember's transmission, as to the urgency of the need for action, but not with Yarborough. He didn't get his case of beer, but I did buy him a few after the flight, as we discussed the problem of verbosity and lack of emotion in threatening situations.

Although interdicting traffic on the trails was our primary mission, in the summer of 1968 we temporarily moved the operation to Saigon, due to the monsoon season moving into Laos.

CHAPTER 10

Saigon

Temporarily leaving the trails was a relief to a degree, as the combat environment was greatly eased, and it gave us the opportunity to use the Gunship in the manner it was developed to be used, for the support of troops in contact.

As you may or may not know, the "secret" war in Laos was waged and controlled by the Air Force, while the war in Viet Nam was waged and controlled by the Army. The Gunship was originally developed as a close air support system for troops in contact with the enemy in the war in South Vietnam. The Gunship, however, proved to be such a successful truck killer on the trails that the Air Force wanted to keep it there. The monsoon season greatly affected our operation in Laos, thus the change. Unfortunately, the monsoon season didn't seem to faze the enemy, and they were able to greatly increase their defensive firepower by moving in more AAA weaponry.

We could tell by the generations of improvements (the size of our gunship weapons, type of sensors developed, operating altitudes etc.) that the political arguments by the Air Force were winning out. Nonetheless, we had the opportunity, if only for a few months, to work with troops in contact almost on a nightly basis. A point in evidence, we never used the four 7.62 millimeter mini guns on the trails. The 5500 ft. operating altitude was too high for them to be effective, since the rounds would simply tumble and would not penetrate and explode upon contact like the 20 Millimeter Vulcan rounds. The 7.62 were primarily used for killing personnel. In Vietnam, we operated at a 3500 ft. altitude and they were very effective. In addition, their tracers were psychologically effective against the enemy, but, on the trails all they did was give our position away and draw AAA. On the trails, it was "kill or be killed." In country, the threat was nowhere so great. It was search and destroy, provide close air support, aid and assist, rescue, and join in on the big and small firefights (I'm not talking "Smokey-the-bear type firefighting.") This was by far the more enjoyable of the two missions, and most of the "funny" anecdotes come from this campaign.

Arriving in Saigon, we were billeted in a small hotel down a long alley. We had to walk the last 200 yards down the alley due to road construction. Sometimes after flying into the early morning hours, those 200 yards seemed like a mile, not because we were tired, but because the alley was dark, and we were in a city, where your barber by day with a razor to your throat could turn into a Viet Cong soldier at night with an AK-47. We had security guards at the hotel, but we never knew what might be waiting for us in that alley. We were staying in the hotel one night when a 122 mm rocket shell came whistling in and destroyed the building next to ours. We didn't think they were after us personally, as those attacks were launched from miles away, and the rockets were at the mercy of the winds, etc. The enemy usually fired only one round from a given site, fleeing immediately before they could be located by a FAC (forward air controller) or gunship that might be up. It was difficult getting to sleep that night, wondering, "what if tonight was different" or "what if they decided to launch another round and the winds were a little different?"

I remember spending my afternoons on the flat roof of this hotel studying my Command and Staff correspondence course and listening to the war going on all around me.

After a few weeks, we moved to another hotel. Once again, this hotel was down an alley. However, we could drive our vehicle all the way to the hotel. It, too, had armed guards around it, but this was the hotel that was overrun by the enemy three times during our stay. Fortunately for our aircrew, we were always flying during the attacks. Our ground support personnel, however, were there, as this was the time we were flying three missions a night: four hours up to Danang, then to the DMZ to search for helicopters that were reported to be skirting the DMZ out over the ocean and inserting North Vietnamese. We would return to Danang, refuel, and then fly 4 hours back to Saigon. We did this for many days, leaving Saigon at 4:00 p.m. and arriving back at about 7:00 a.m. the next morning, so our support troops were in the hotel during those nights. We did not have any of them killed or wounded, since they were able to get to the top floor during the attack (where their guns and ammo were stored). However, the security guards were killed on each occasion. Quick response by the South Vietnamese army personnel prevented further personnel losses.

I remember one night after a regular mission, Tom Sparr and I were driving back to the hotel in our pickup. Three shadowy black clad figures appeared on the road carrying weapons, and flagged us down. I was really upset when Tom stopped. I thought they were Viet Cong and probably would do us in. Thinking back, I guess Tom had no option but to stop or they might have mowed us down. When we stopped, they all jumped in the back of the pickup, and banged on the top of the cab. Tom started driving. We didn't know where to drive to, so I suggested we continue heading for the hotel. We did just that. You can imagine how frightened we were when after a while the men banged on the cab again. We thought that this was going to be the place where something happened or our route was about to be changed. The figures jumped out of the back and disappeared off the side of the road. We just sat there wondering what was going to happen next. I'll tell you what was going to happen next: we got the hell out of there, leaving tire tracks and dust behind. We never did find out what that was about. All I know was that we were in the logistics business for a short time that night, moving troops of some kind from someplace to somewhere. I often wondered, if they were enemy soldiers, what would have been their reaction if they later found out that they had the two AC-130 pilots within their grasp. Along those same lines, I always wondered why the Viet Cong never attempted to rocket or satchel charge our aircraft. We always parked it in the same revetment (Yankee 13) on the C-130 parking ramp. It sat there all day long, every day. Since it was the only AC-130 at the time, blowing it up would have really been a coup for their side. They never tried. Maybe they thought we were too smart to park it in the same place all the time. Maybe we figured they would think that way.

Shortly after the attacks on our hotel, the Air Force, in all its wisdom, decided to move us on base for housing. We settled in to barracks just behind the morgue. The morgue operated 24 hours and the large noisy ventilating fans required getting used to. The odors weren't that good either.

When we first arrived in Saigon, the Army gave us a Special Forces Major who flew with us so we could learn the geographical aspects and landmarks, and help coordinate radio communications with combat units on the ground. This was an almost impossible task, since inter-service communications was probably the weakest link we encountered during those days. This was well before the establishment of the Joint Service Operations Command (JSOC).

The Major's name was Don Faircloth, but he referred to himself as "Casper the friendly ghost." He figured that the AC-47's were called Spooky, we were named Spectre, and therefore Casper was quite appropriate.

I will never forget the night we were working along the north side of Black Virgin Mountain in central South Vietnam and had located what we were told were North Vietnamese tanks. This was unusual in that at this time of the conflict, North Vietnamese tanks had never been spotted that far south. I believed they were friendly forces whose location had not been correctly identified. Nonetheless, we were given permission to fire on them. I wasn't overly concerned because we only had HEI (High Explosive Incendiary) rounds for the 20 mm, and not API (Armor Piercing Incendiary) rounds. If the tanks were ours, the most damage we could do was to probably scare the "you know what" out of them. I was not sure the HEI would penetrate the enemy's armor or not.

As it turned out it was a moot point (possibly divine intervention). We had such high winds swirling around the mountain, that I was having one hell of a time hitting them. I felt at the time that I couldn't hit a bull in the ass with a bass fiddle. We were all getting somewhat frustrated when Bob Dunham called on the interphone, "Bob, you're not going to believe this, but Casper has just emptied his service revolver out the left parachute door trying to kill those tanks." Now that's what I call frustration. Because of our 3500 ft. altitude and over 5000 ft. slant range distance, my guess that Casper might have only killed some Viet Cong friendly monkeys.

We had another time when some marines didn't fully understand the capabilities of their weapon system, nor of ours. This was during the time we were working north out of Danang trying to stop helicopter infiltration by sea around the DMZ. We were a part of a task force, and our operations officer met with other elements each morning in Saigon to discuss the results of the previous night's work. One night when our Ops officer was flying with us on the mission, we were approaching the DMZ (demilitarized zone) from the ocean when we were picked up by a strong search light which appeared to be located right on the DMZ. I turned back to the ocean and attempted another approach. Again we were bathed in the search light's beam. Not knowing whether the source of the beam was friendly or what kind of AAA might be associated with it, I decided to break off the approach and circumnavigate the area to search farther along the DMZ. The next morning at the briefing, a Marine Major reported that they had successfully thwarted an attempt by a large aircraft to penetrate the DMZ. He reported that the aircraft had turned around. When our Ops officer, a Lt. Colonel, who had been on board, told him that it had been us that they had prevented from accomplishing our goal, the Major puffed up with an air of superiority saying, "It was a good thing that you didn't come any closer, because you would have been shot down as they had quad 50's mounted around that search light." Our commander agreed saying that "Yes, it was a good thing that we had broken off our approach." He explained further that our rules of engagement allow us to return fire at anything that shoots at us, and that we ate quad 50's for breakfast. This was true as the quad 50's rounds were pretty much spent by the time they reached our altitude, and that all they were good for was to highlight our target. The Marine was obviously not aware that we were in country, what we were, and what would have been coming down on his troops had they dared engage.

Although this was somewhat humorous, the sad thing was that with the lack of inter-service communications in general and a lack of complete knowledge of the whereabouts of friendly forces, there is no doubt there were a few incidences of friendly fire damage from different sources. I remember one time in particular we were given permission to fire on an encampment because Army Headquarters was sure there were no friendlies in the area. I noticed the encampment made no indication they were afraid of our presence, no fleeing vehicles, no snuffed out fires, no tracers headed our way, but still permission came to fire on the target. I came back in the firing configuration and, although not completely sure we were not going to fire on friendlies, I decided to make a 360-degree circle around the encampment. It turned out to be the best decision I made while a gunship pilot. During the 360 turn, we received a frantic radio call yelling, "Hold Fire, Hold Fire." They informed us that they had made a mistake and that the encampment was indeed friendly.

You can imagine my heartbeat about that time. It helped me develop a philosophy that I used thereafter. If in doubt, as I had been that time, I would fire my first rounds close, but not on target. I figured that since everyone knew the American forces and their allies' maintained air superiority over South Vietnam and that only friendly aircraft would be overhead, we wouldn't receive return fire. Yes, I do understand the flaw in this strategy, but let's keep it a secret from the enemy. It is possible that my making the 360 degree pylon turn created a suspicion in the friendlies, that like the AC47 Puff, we might be a gunship of some kind and they contacted their control agency.

One night we were called in to support a village that was being overrun. The local mayor was on the radio and put me through a marksmanship test before he would allow me to bring my fire in close enough to save his ass. He had me fire into a line of trees far away from his position. He then had me take out some closer trees. Then he had me take out a specific tree. He finally gave me the go ahead to work in and around specific buildings in his village, where he claimed the VC were hiding. He was very specific about me not hitting his boat, a pleasure launch tied up at the pier. I often wondered if the particular houses he directed me to hit did in fact contain VC, or maybe it was a way to ensure his re-election the next year by getting rid of his competition.

Another funny story about a village mayor involved our arrival on a minor skirmish where a local had been wounded and we were requested to call in a "dust off" (an emergency medical evacuation Huey helicopter). We contacted the Huey, whose altitude and distance precluded him from having direct radio contact with the mayor. The "dust off" asked me to ask the mayor where the wounded man had been hit. I passed the message to the mayor. His answer was that the wounded man had been hit "here," (meaning his location). I repeated that the army corpsman needed to know just where the man had been hit. The mayor insisted that he had been hit "here." I tried to simplify the message by saying, "The doctor needs to know just where the man had been wounded (apparently not much of an improvement). The mayor then stated in a somewhat irritated tone, "You (meaning me) come down here and I will show you just where he was hit." (So much for clear communicating.)

On 25 Sept. 1968, we were flying a typical mission. Tom Sparr was in the left seat and I was in the right. Lt.Col. Koeninger was flying with us. We were just about out of fuel when we got a distress call from the Special Forces camp at Thein Ngon. It seems that the enemy was fast approaching and they feared a big firefight. We responded, but it was pretty quiet, so we decided to head back to Saigon to refuel and rearm. In route, we lost a DC generator. Before we got out of radio range, the camp at Thein Ngon contacted us and said the siege had begun. We raced back to Saigon where the flight engineer and I changed the generator on the engine while the rest of the crewmembers refueled and rearmed. We headed back, and this time I was in the left seat. While we were on the ground, a heavy line of thunderstorms moved in between Thein Ngon and us. We were able to pick our way around and even through some of the lightest areas. When we arrived at the camp, the firefight had fully developed. Tracer rounds were coming out from the compound, trip flares were going off around the outer perimeter defense, mortar rounds were going off inside the compound. We were able to pick up some muzzle flashes from small arms or mortars, but for the most part, we had to be selective in targets, not knowing where the friendlies were located. I asked the outpost if they had any ballgames out (a term for patrols). They had some, but were confident in describing their locations.

One of the advantages of the 7.62 cal. mini guns was their inability to completely penetrate the bunker sandbags and roofs. I told the compound commander to get all of his people "under the umbrella." This was a recognized term that meant to take cover wherever you were, but under something the 7.62 could not penetrate, such as sand bagged bunkers. Although the 7.62 rounds could ricochet, they would not explode like the 20 mms. While he was directing the umbrella tactic, I worked the perimeter, firing at muzzle flashes and possible mortar launch areas. Since the enemy had penetrated the outer defense, trip flares going off also indicated areas of high probability of enemy penetration routes. Moving his troops under cover caused them to cease firing, which resulted in the enemies taking advantage of the lull to infiltrate in great numbers. I pulled off, as if leaving the area. I waited about 5 minutes to return to what appeared to be a quiet battlefield. Fortunately, the ploy had worked. The compound advised that the place was crawling with VC/NVA soldiers openly approaching across the firing zones. The compound assured me that all of the troops were under the umbrella. You can guess what happened next. You may not know the capability of a 7.62 mini gun (of which we had four). Each gun is capable of putting a round in every square ft. of a football field in a matter of seconds. They also have the psychological advantage of being tracer ammunition. Talk about a rain of fire; I quickly saturated the entire compound area. A follow up report described 145 killed. This did not account for the bodies and wounded the enemy were able to carry off into Cambodia. Over 100 assorted enemy weapons were recovered and several anti-aircraft positions were destroyed. These figures come from the Vietnamese Cross of Gallantry orders we were given.

There was quite a bit of 50 Caliber AAA, but for the most part, it was ineffective, with one particular exception. As we were about ready to depart, they had dispatched an AC-47 to replace us. As we were operating blacked out, Lt.Col. Koeninger decided to reach over my shoulder and turn on the anti-collision light so that the AC-47 could see us. Well, the AC-47 did see us, but so did a nearby 50-caliber battery that hadn't been involved in our scrimmage because it wasn't near the compound, opened up on us. Since we flew in 360-degree turns, our path just happened to fly right over his position, which put us well within his range. We took quite a lacing. However, the battery was apparently unaware that we fired out of the left side of the aircraft. I continued the 360 turn, and fortunately, the fifty calibers kept on firing giving me a good target to enable me to blow them to kingdom come.

I have often wondered whether I would have been awarded the Silver Star for that mission if Col. Koeninger hadn't turned on that anti-collision light.

There were many other skirmishes and firefights where we got to highlight the capabilities of the aircraft. On several occasions, because of our special night sensors, we were able to work in such close proximity with our troops that they had to whisper on their radios to keep from being discovered by the enemy. One soldier said that I had followed his directions so closely that I had killed enemy troops within 25 yards of his position.

The attempted overrun of the Special Forces troops at Katum is an example. I was able to fire with such pinpoint accuracy, that although the Katum mission was earlier, the body count mimicked the mission at Thein Ngon. I was awarded the Distinguished Flying Cross for that one. The reason for the difference in the award was that I didn't navigate through thunderstorms to get there, physically change a DC generator between flights, use the "under the umbrella tactic," and - probably the most influencing - I didn't have Lt.Col. Koeninger turning on the anti-collision beacon, revealing our position, and resulting in our "getting laced" by antiaircraft fire.

When the monsoon season was over, we returned to Ubon. This was an exciting and somewhat harrowing time. More of our replacement crews had arrived with more airplanes and needed training in actual combat and, to further frustrate the situation, the enemy had moved many more AAA batteries onto the trails to include more SAMs (surface to air missiles).

In addition to this, our requirement for overhead cover increased, due to the added aircraft and increased AAA. This meant more F-4 coverage. By now our reputation and, more importantly, the high BDA totals for the 497 Night Owls spread, and many other F-4 squadrons wanted to get in on the spoils. This resulted in loss of the ability to brief and debrief our overhead cover because they were coming from other bases.

By the time I left, we had increased by four to five more gunships and eight more crews. Due to the increased flights and, to some degree the inexperience of the crews, the AAA damage to our aircraft increased significantly. Also, I was fortunate in that the shoulder-fired surface to air missiles hadn't been used on the trails during my tour.

CHAPTER 11

On to Germany

Near the end of my gunship tour we were allowed to offer suggestions for our next assignment. Tom Sparr, one of our original pilots, had served a tour as a pilot in the 7406 support squadron at Rhein-Main Air Base, Germany. The unit was a little known special operations squadron with a highly classified mission. Their aircraft commanders had to have at least 4000 hours in the C-130. Since I qualified, I applied and was accepted as an aircraft commander.

Being a senior Captain, my promotion board was meeting at this time. While on leave at Dottie's home in Ft. Lauderdale, Florida, I received a tubular package from the Air Force. Opening it, I was surprised to learn that I had been awarded the Silver Star Medal for Gallantry for the mission at Thein Ngon Special Forces camp that I described at length earlier, and the Distinguished Flying Cross for a similar mission at Katum Special Forces Camp. The medals themselves were included in the package as well as the certificates.

I contacted the personnel department at San Antonio, Texas, to ensure these were included in my promotion folder along with my certification for completion of my Air Command and Staff correspondence course. They informed me that the Education Shop at Ubon hadn't forwarded that information and, unfortunately, the Silver Star Medal couldn't be entered into my record until it had been formally presented by a General Officer. This was indeed bad news, since my promotion board was in session.

Dottie, Robbie, and I proceeded on to Germany. As luck would have it, we were immediately assigned quarters. I say "as luck would have it" because since I was number one on the housing list, they assigned us to a set of quarters that had been turned in early, but would be undergoing renovation and wouldn't be ready for a couple of months. While we waited in the hotel, other quarters became available, but they would not change our quarters. Therefore, junior officers got into better quarters sooner, as they became available sooner. I fought the civilian housing authorities very hard, but in Deutschland, "orders are orders." So, we spent four wonderful years in a renovated large fourth floor walkup (no elevator) twelve-family stairwell unit. Dottie became pregnant while we were in the hotel, so now we had two babies in diapers, with the unit laundry located in the basement of the stairwell. Between diapers, groceries, all purchases, and just coming and going, often carrying two children, we both developed strong calf muscles, especially Dottie, as I spent a good bit of time away from home flying and TDY to Athens. One positive aspect was that the beer deliverer brought the cases of flip top bottles of beer all the way up to our door.

The heartbreak of our stay in the hotel was that one morning while having breakfast at the Officer's club, a friend announced that the new Majors list was in the Air Force Times. When I checked, my name was not on it. Adding to the disappointment was that we later found out that none of my medals were in my promotion folder at the time the selection board met, as I said before, because they hadn't been presented by a General Officer; neither was my Command and Staff graduation certificate. I pleaded to the promotions section at the personnel center at Randolph AFB, but was told nothing could be done about it. Thankfully, now they have changed the policy, and a review is allowed.

Now for the last of the bad news, we learned later that there would not be a Majors board the following year, putting me two years behind my peers. I will add that the four-star Commander of USAFE (United States Air Forces in Europe) General Holzapple, had a big military parade and ceremony at Wiesbaden Air Base to present my medals shortly after my "non-selection" to Major.

The remaining four years were fantastic. Our son Rick was born in

1970. Therefore, he held dual citizenship until he decided before turning eighteen whether he wanted to become German or American. Fortunately, he chose to become an American.

Due to being passed-over, I elected to continue my education by earning my Master's degree from Ball State University. I got my records straightened out and was selected for Major, two years late.

We brought Dottie's Porsche with us to Germany and participated in sports car rallies throughout the country.

We bought a new Volkswagen camper, and traveled and camped all over Europe. We sold it four years later for more than we paid for it.

We enjoyed skiing in Austria, Switzerland, and Germany. Even Robbie learned to ski in Austria. I was ski captain for one club ski trip, so we had our expenses paid by the club.

Both of our families came to visit, including my daughters Cindy and Karen, as well as my Aunt Ruth from Boston. We were able to take Dottie's mom and dad to Oktoberfest in Munich. My dad visited the Holy Land while Mom and Aunt Ruth traveled around Europe.

One of the advantages of being there at that time was the fact the exchange rate was so good: four German Marks to each US dollar. Added to this was that the big military furniture storage house burned down causing USAFE to allow us to buy furniture on the German market to use and then take with us upon return to the US. Because of this, they had to increase our moving weight allowances, which led us to bring back more.

Due to government fiscal restraints that came into effect while we were still there, all three-year tours to Germany were involuntary extended to four years. (Boo-Hoo).

As for my job, due to classification, there isn't much I can say about the mission other than the fact we flew as hard crews: always the same crewmembers, including two navigators. We flew along Soviet borders as long and as high as possible, which meant eleven-hour missions at altitudes where we had to have our helmets on and oxygen masks at the side of our faces. The missions were hours and hours of true boredom interrupted by moments of stark terror.

In addition to being an aircraft commander, an additional duty was that of scheduling officer -- assigning crews to missions. All crews, including mine, spent 10 days out of each month flying out of Athens Greece, especially good in summer, bad in winter. We spent so much time there, that some of us joined the Glyfada golf club.

I was fortunate enough to be able to take my family to Athens for a month while I flew missions. Our rented apartment was right across from the beach, so Dottie and boys could enjoy the beach while I flew.

Glyfada was a sleepy little fishing village when we were there. Dottie and I returned many years later as tourists, and it had turned into a thriving city, with high rises, a commuter train, and flourishing businesses. The small Greek restaurant "George's Steak House" which we had previously visited almost on a daily basis, was still there. It was a lot larger, and since he had been elderly back in the early 70's, I figured George himself had been long gone, but his son might still be around. We were told that the son would return soon, so we waited to talk with him and tell him how grateful we were for George's friendship. We had rented our apartment from him when I had brought the family down for a month twenty years earlier. The son was very appreciative of our comments, and then asked if we would like to talk with George, as he would be coming in for his daily ritual of meeting and dining with guests as he had been doing for decades. We did, he came, and we dined and drank. I drank the creosote-tasting Retsina that we drank for 22 cents a carafe back in the early 70's, just to commemorate the occasion.

George had taken us octopus fishing and talked us into joining the Glyfada golf club so we could play golf with him on our off days.

While I am on a sidetrack to Glyfada, I should mention the political climate at the time. The Greek revolution was in the air, and one New Year's Eve, my crew and I were having dinner at the "Congo Palace," which was the US Officers club at the time. We were seated at the back of the dining room next to the wall that separated the dining room from the small BX (Base Exchange). A terrorist group had planted a bomb in the air conditioning space in the BX, and it went off. We were not injured, but it did put an end to our New Year's Eve dinner. In fact, I think we ended up drinking our dinner.

On one occasion we were prevented from flying back to Germany on schedule. I was taxiing out and was instructed to "hold in place." A commercial airliner had been hijacked and was sitting on the tarmac. They surmised that any movement by a military aircraft might result in a desperate reaction from the hijackers. We deplaned and waited them out. The situation was resolved peacefully, I assume, and we continued our mission home.

Now that I have completed the little sojourn to Glyfada, I will continue with my Rhein-Main meanderings. After about 18 months, I was moved to Squadron Standardization Evaluation, giving annual and no-notice check-rides to aircrews, replacing Bill Brooks, who was assigned to the gunship program at UBON. Unfortunately, he and his crew were lost over Laos.

I was later moved to wing Stan-Eval. Coming off regular flying schedule gave me more time to complete my Master's degree in Counseling from Ball State University, and be selected to participate in a new Air Force program. There will be more detail about the assignment later.

Rhein Main Rockets, Continental Sports conference champions and the entire United States Air Force in Europe (USAFE) Champions 1972-73. I'm in the back row, second from the left.

American football is very popular with the military overseas. I was asked if I would be the head coach for the Rhein-Main high school football team. We competed against other high school teams from other services.

I guess I impressed someone, because the next year they wanted me to be the backfield coach and one of two offensive coordinators for the Rhein-Main Rockets.

As I said, American football is very popular in Europe and every Air Force base had a team. The Army dropped their teams, so we even had some Army players. There were two conferences in the USAFE (US Air Forces Europe), The Continental Sports Conference that included all German bases and bases located in Spain, and the United Kingdom conference that included all the bases in England.

The teams were similar to semi pro teams. We had a few ex-pros, many ex-college standouts, including one Small-College All-American on our team, and many frustrated high school standouts. We had officers and enlisted team members. I might add here that our Wing Commander Colonel Tom Sadler was quite involved in recruiting experienced football players from the new arrivals at Rhein-Main and the assigned Army personnel in the area.

Because of our home-away schedule, the team flew to some bases in Spain, and because of our winning the Continental Sports division championship, we flew to England to play for the entire USAFE championship against Upper Hayfield. We weren't   this time.

Fortunately, due to player talent and obviously good coaching, we won the USAFE championship.

After four wonderful years in Germany filled with camping, skiing, golf, tennis, sports car rallies, Oktoberfests, traveling all over Europe, wine and beer festivals, antique collecting, and you name it, it all had to come to an end.

It wasn't a bad deal, as I had mentioned, my being passed over for Major resulting in the two-year delay to Major, allowed me to pursue a Master's degree. Since my major in college had been psychology, I opted to pursue the master's degree in counseling from Ball State University. Ball State, located in Muncie, Indiana, would send over campus Ph.D. professors for our courses. It was not the easiest thing to do, due to my flying and TDY. I spent a lot of time studying while flying. This was allowed, as we had five crewmembers in the cockpit and with two pilots, two navigators and a flight engineer. Yes, eleven-hour missions permitted such diversions (even napping). Class attendance could be affected, so sometimes Dottie would attend, using a tape recorder and taking notes. She was able to do this using as babysitters our German housekeeper or trading off with neighbors wives, whose husbands were also taking advanced degrees.

CHAPTER 12

Back in the States Beale AFB
and The Rated Supplement

The Air Force had decided to add a Social Actions career field to the personnel career tracts. The Social Actions program consisted of three divisions, Race relations, Drug and Alcohol abuse, and Equal Opportunity Treatment. Also during this time, they had adopted what they called the Rated Supplement, which required all pilots to take a break from the cockpit to broaden their Air Force knowledge and management skills over a four-year period. The Air Force was not very happy with the direction the Social Actions program was proceeding and its acceptance by the general Air Force population, as some commanders had used this opportunity to rid their ranks of outspoken zealous minority personnel which were not supportive of the true goals of acceptance and toleration between races.

Apparently, some personnel-type felt that a highly decorated white pilot could help bridge the gap. I was selected to fill such a position, and was assigned to the position of Social Actions Director at the highly prestigious 9th Strategic Reconnaissance Wing which flew the fastest aircraft in the world, the SR71. As Chief of Social Action, I had a staff of instructors and an administrative assistant. My job was primarily managing staff, resolving Equal Opportunity complaints, teaching classes, and inventorying base minority products in the Base Exchange and Commissary. I developed programs and gave briefings on Equal Opportunity, drug and alcohol abuse, and race relations (later named

Human Relations). Additionally, I served on the staffs of the 9th Strategic Reconnaissance Wing, the 456th Bombardment Wing, and the Base Commander. Attending daily staff meetings took a significant amount of my time.

During this period I traveled on the 15th Air Force Inspector General's team, renovated and moved into a new stand-alone Social Actions building. I was checked out for and flew the two-engine C-131 aircraft (the SAC Valley Courier) mission to maintain my Rated Supplement flying status. How I found time to play flag football, golf, tennis, and ski while maintaining a great family life, I will never know.

We enjoyed our tour at Beale, and managed to work in skiing at Lake Tahoe on a regular basis, also playing golf and tennis.

Since my job required us to live on base, we decided to invest in a beautiful ten acres just outside Nevada City, California. Nevada City was a quaint old gold mining town, and a true tourist attraction. We paid $15,000 for the acreage and sold it six years later for $100,000

Apparently, my performance impressed several General Officers, as The Strategic Air Command decided to add a Social Actions Inspector to the SAC Inspector General Team at SAC headquarters, and guess who was assigned as the first Social Actions officer to serve on the team?

This required our family to move to Offutt AFB near Omaha, Nebraska where we purchased our first home since our marriage in Belleview, Nebraska.

We enjoyed our tour at SAC headquarters, but the IG position required much Temporary Duty (TDY) flying all over the country and the world making surprise weeklong inspection visits to SAC bases. If you saw the movie "Gathering of Eagles" with Rock Hudson, you got somewhat of an idea what a SAC IG inspection was like and how it could affect the careers of many senior officers. I had several duties once the team made our unexpected arrival at each SAC AF Base. My first stop was a surprise visit to the base social actions office. I remember arriving at one office where the entire staff including the Chief of Social Actions had decided to take the whole day off to attend a big boxing match in New York City. That was bad enough, but compounding their problem was the fact that they had forgotten to lock the office which left me access to all their files.

You can imagine their perplexity and surprise when I showed up early the next morning with a handful of write-ups. Other problems in the office came to light during the week and it came as no surprise to their Wing Commander when I gave the entire program an unsatisfactory grade. It also came as no surprise to the Chief of Social Actions when he found himself looking for another job after our departure.

One of the fun duties I had was to "rob" different facilities on the bases such as the BX, the officers or NCO clubs, the base liquor store, etc. I would hand the cashier a card saying this was a simulated robbery, and they were to perform their emergency robbery procedures. Our security police inspectors would be monitoring the whole base's response. I was quite innovative in my escape and evasion tactics. One time I had disguised myself and my accomplice in tennis gear, and we spent the period after the robbery playing tennis on the courts next to the officers club while the security police and the base searched for us. Another time after robbing the base liquor store, and having left our military pickup in front of the store, we raised our hood and flagged down a base security police car responding to the robbery alarm. We convinced the driver that being inspector general team members we needed transportation to the main gate. You can imagine the expression on the face of our senior security police inspector when we entered the gate building and I winked at him.

Upon our team's arrival, surveys were passed out to base personnel. My duty was to collect and read the surveys which requested opinions about morale and human relations on the base. I would respond as necessary. These surveys did not need to be signed. However, one navigator assigned to the base chose to sign his and had started his comments by saying, "Since I know no one will actually read this, I am going to sign my comments." I happened to recognize the name as being one of my good friends in the squadron in Germany. I went to the plans office where he worked. He had his back to the door when I entered. I threw my cap on his desk saying with a loud voice, "So you think no one reads the SAC surveys." Without turning around he shouted, "Bob

Reneau, you old SOB, what the hell are you doing here?"

I also had the duty to do equal opportunity and race relations investigations during the week as well as proof read individual inspector's comments for the report and team brief out at the end of the inspection. Fortunately, th e team chief and our briefing Colonel had good proofing skills to back me up. At the end of the tour on the SAC IG team, I was promoted to Lieutenant Colonel.

On the home front, we were involved in many activities: golf, tennis, hobnobbing with senior SAC officers and families, and soccer. I became a soccer coach and had two undefeated seasons. Dottie was the team mother and we supported two teams, since both boys played. We purchased, renovated, and managed a four-bedroom apartment unit in downtown Belleview.

CHAPTER 13

Back to the "Herc"

The Air Force personnel center contacted me saying the Air Force was in desperate need of highly experienced C-130 pilots, and since my rated supplement tour was completed, they said they would send me to any C-130 base of my choice. I opted for Pope AFB next to Ft. Bragg in Fayetteville, NC, knowing that if I selected any other base, I would be spending lots of TDY time at Pope without my family. We purchased a home on Haverhill Drive in the Devonwood subdivision close to Ft. Bragg and Pope AFB. The boys convinced us to put in a 20x40 in-ground swimming pool. I even got them to sign a contract agreeing to take care of the pool cleaning and the chemical upkeep. (Lesson to self: Never sign a contract without a penalty for non-performance!) What was I to do, dig out the pool and replant the trees? Rob and Rick learned a lesson from that. They don't make contracts with their kids without including a penalty clause. I, too, learned a lesson and have not written or signed any contracts without such a clause.

While on the subject of swimming pools, I had better tell the true version of this story before it is perverted, as it already has been, by two individuals of my immediate offspring who insist on telling their version. I had a riding lawn mower and was cutting the grass around the pool. We had decorator timbers beside our deck out to the pool that had grass growing on a four-foot wide area between the timbers. I backed the lawn mower into the area and the left drive wheel came over the timber and stranded the lawn mower. I got off the lawn mower to lift the left rear wheel back up onto the grassy area. Now remember, I was a highly qualified pilot at the time and immediately resolved the problem.

However, this highly qualified pilot had neglected to put the lawn mower into neutral gear. Now lawn mowers, like teen agers, have a mind of their own, and this rebellious lawnmower headed straight for the pool. Thinking swiftly, I jumped onto the lawn mower to turn it away from the pool. Not being fully aware of the not-so-short turning radius of the lawn mower, that renegade managed to go over the side with me on board. Being the quick thinker, I managed to leap clear of the mower, but not before it and I landed in the pool. There is more to the story. My teenaged son Rob was napping in the family room and after a few very loud shouts from me he emerged onto the deck. I was still in the pool and yelled for him to get the water hose connected to a nearby hose bib. His brilliant reply was, "Why? The pool already has enough water in it."

My response was, "Just throw it to me."

He did, with a questioning look on his nap-interrupted face. I dove to the bottom of the pool, wrapped the hose around the steering wheel of the mower, resurfaced and told him to disconnect the hose from the house and walk it to the shallow end of the pool where we met, each with an end of hose in hand. We then pulled the mower up to the shallow edge and pulled it up on the pool decking. I was able to start it but it did not run for very long. The boys end their story with me ending up in the pool after driving the mower into it. I prefer the full version, revealing my quick thinking and a somewhat dumb statement from Rob.

At Pope, I was assigned to the 41st Tactical Airlift Squadron as the "Chief Pilot." As such, I was responsible for managing all the Squadron pilots. This was during a time when all C-130 squadrons pulled rotational duty at Mildenhall Air Base in England for several months at a time. The 41st TAS pulled their tour in the spring of 1977. While at Mildenhall, we participated in exercise Long-link. This was a great opportunity to discuss tactics, fly, compete athletically, and socialize (party) with a sister squadron (70 squadron) of the Royal Air Force.

I was given the hardship duty (right!) of taking two aircraft and three crews to participate in the event. The RAF had invited some of the young squadron wives who had joined their husbands for their tour at Mildenhall, to join on the Long-link festivities.

We thought we would spice up our arrival at RAF Lyneham by attaching drogue parachutes to the ramps of both aircraft and deploy them in unison on landing, roll, taxi in in close formation, and simultaneously shut down engines at the exact Greenwich Mean Time of our scheduled arrival. This entire procedure was of course a ruse, as we never use fighter drogue chutes to slow us down on landing, because all of our engines are fully reversible in order to stop in amazingly short landing distances, as are the RAF C-130s. When we deplaned, we were met by the RAF distinguished arrival hosts (all qualified aircrew members) with a typical stiff-upper-lip tongue-in-cheek comment, "Very interesting." One of the goals of this exercise was to exchange tactical operations techniques. This began a fun and frivolous-filled week of flying, touring, sports competing, discussing tactics, and partying. Mostly the latter.

Our first official act was to present the 70th squadron with a young sapling North Carolina Dogwood tree that we jointly planted in the squadron operations building yard.

Our first unofficial act was to attend a big party that evening at the squadron commander's home off base. Our senior loadmaster (who will go unnamed in order to protect the guilty), managed to break the Loo seat (toilet seat) in the residence.

The next day I arranged for the desk attendant at the Officer's mess to go into the village to purchase a new Loo seat. He was to leave it behind the desk. I picked it up a couple of days later and painted our large squadron patch on the top lid.

During this time, a member of the British Royal family visited the base to present an award to one of the squadrons. I was invited to attend the formal dinner to welcome her and got the chance to meet her.

Let me jump forward to our last night's dinner and party. When I got up to speak, I invited the loadmaster to join me on stage. I broke out the newly decorated Loo seat. I opened the lid, placed it over his head, and dubbed him "The Earl of Loo." There was a great round of laughter from both squadrons when I explained the circumstance associated with the presentation, but not before I heard a loud female gasp from those assembled. A woman approached me after the short talk and demanded to know where I had obtained the Loo seat. I told her that I had asked the desk clerk to purchase it for me and leave it behind the desk, where I had picked it up. How was I to know that I had apparently absconded with the seat of a member the Royal family? The squadron unknowingly took the decorated Loo seat and hung it on a wall in the squadron briefing room. I learned later that some official-appearing men came to the squadron within a few days and left with a slightly oval package.

L to R: Princess Anne, unnamed lady, Lt Col Reneau

To this day in my doddering and often mischievous mind, I can't help wondering if the Royalty carried their own Loo seats with them in order to prevent catching diseases or spreading them. (I'll bet this does not get by the editor.)

Among the tours the Squadron gave us was a low-level tour of Scotland terminating in two choices. We could either visit a scotch distillery or play golf on the Royal and Ancient Saint Andrews golf course. I, being an avid golfer at the time, would have loved to play the golf course. However, being the senior officer, I decided the responsible choice was to accompany the young officers and enlisted men to the distillery. Who knows what could have happened turning a bunch of young "YANK" crewmembers loose for hours in a small Scotland village. I guess in the end it was a wise decision, as I no longer play golf, but still drink scotch. Besides, it gives me the opportunity to tell my golfing buddies the story and watch them shake their heads and wonder about my mental faculties.

We had sports competitions with the Brits during our stay. Upon our departure, we made a low pass over their squadron operations building and air-dropped a drogue-chuted load onto their volleyball court. To this day, my dear friend Ken Foster claims we missed the court and the chute landed in an adjoining fuel storage area.

The Long-link program requires that we reciprocate visits, so 70 Squadron with several of their wives joined us at Pope Air Force Base for more training, fun, and frivolity. We took the wives onto a large parachute drop zone where they were fairly up-close and personal to the landing paratroopers. Watching the troopers slowly drifting down, one of the Brit wives shouted out "If I catch one, can I keep him"? I love the British sense of "humour."

Since this was a reciprocal visit, I should mention that one of the Brits walked through and completely took out a patio screen door at a party in the home of our Operations Officer. I guess that is tit-for-tat, eye-for-eye, or screen door-for-Loo seat.

One of our young co-pilots had worked at Disneyworld as a steam engine engineer before coming on active duty. He still had some connections, and was able to arrange for a large group to attend the park. Our regulations wouldn't allow us to fill up our planes with civilians for a trip to Disneyworld, but fortunately the Brit squadron commander had the authority to do so with his planes. We loaded our families, the Brit wives, and offered remaining seats to other Pope AFB personnel and took off in two RAF C-130s to Orlando for the day.

During their visit, we held a nice dinner party at a hotel in Fayetteville, NC. The hotel had a swimming pool, so obviously we had a swimming relay race between the Brits and the Yanks. We felt we had a good chance of winning, since two of us were university swimmers. My dear friend Foster was quite confident they could beat us. The victor is still in dispute. The teams were neck and neck when it came down to the two final swimmers, Ken and me. By the way, the female Mayor of Fayetteville was sitting poolside as a guest at our party. I finished first, but had no idea of what transpired during the race. I touched the finish first and only then did I hear what had happened to Ken. He was quite a ways behind me, swimming in the nude. As he started his racing dive, one of our navigators, (Chuck Leach, to name the guilty) grabbed Ken's "swimming costume" as the Brits call it, completely ripping it from his body. Undaunted and with a stiff upper lip, Ken completed the course. I doubt if he attempted a flip turn at the other end of the pool. A towel was provided for his pool exit and escape. With the aplomb of the perfect English gentleman, he executed a proper bow to the Mayor as he passed her on the edge of the pool on the way to the shower. We still discuss the results and "might-have-beens" concerning the race. As the host (and victor), I graciously ceded the race to the overly-handicapped competitor and dear friend, Ken.

The competition that evening didn't end at poolside. We purchased two very large pewter beer mugs, or tankards, and had them engraved with each squadron's emblem and date of the event. We challenged the Brits to a beer-drinking relay race. The two teams lined up, ran their tankards to the beer kegs, filled to the top and finished the drink, then ran the tanker back to the next guy in line, who would repeat the run and quaff leg. I have drunk beer with the best of them, and next to the Australians, the Brits are the very close second. Knowing this, we had the engraver put in false bottoms on the tankards, but only after filling the empty space of the Brits' with lead, thus adding several pounds to their burden. At the end of the race, we exchanged tankards as squadron keepsakes of the event. I don't know to this day, if they ever learned of, or suspected, the prank. I think it would be somewhat unfair to announce the winners of the race, but as all military personnel know, all is fair in prank or war.

Shortly after our return from England, and after hosting the reciprocating Long-link visit from the Brits, I was assigned to be the commander of the special missions group called Credible Cat. This was a highly classified mission that I commanded for four years. We had four crews and three permanently assigned C-130 aircraft. Our maintenance priority was the highest in the Air Force, and on occasion, I had to use it. This resulted in four years of a perfect on-time delivery date record, flying at least two missions a week. I handpicked all the crewmembers for their experience, reliability, and dedication to complete this extremely important national security mission. All were completely vetted and awarded compartmentalized Top Secret Clearances. Obviously, due to the ongoing nature of the mission, I can't go into a description of it. For those who have read this memoir thus far, this was the most satisfying assignment of my "risk taking" career.

SPECTRE 07

Our stay at Fayetteville and Pope AFB provided the most enjoyable times of our life. Both boys grew up there. Their pool cleaning participation being an exception, they enjoyed all the joys of growing up. Both were outstanding athletes. Both won State Championships in soccer at Fayetteville Academy. Rob was the goalkeeper and the team set a national record and experienced a soccer rule-changing event by participating in a nine sudden-death-overtime state championship game, resulting in an extra 90-minute sudden-death-overtime game. The game was finally terminated in a tie and a dual championship with High Point Wesleyan High. This led to a nationwide end of more than two overtimes in high school soccer. Rob made the NC state championship team and received a soccer scholarship to Appalachian State University. Rick made the winning shot in the next year's state championship game.

Dottie and I coached the boy's travel league teams, and Dottie convinced the 4 Star commander of Ft. Bragg, General McMull, to let her start a woman's soccer league on post for female soldiers and dependent wives. She played on one of the teams and was their leading scorer. Remember that "Ace kicking" tennis player I mentioned in the first chapter of this memoir? She was quite the athlete, and throughout her life, she was the epitome of a true athlete supporter. She never wanted me to call her an athlete supporter, but upon her passing, ASU held a moment of silence in her honor at an Appalachian State basketball game. She had requested and received permission from the ASU athletic department and coaches to start Football 101 and Basketball 101. These were programs where coaches would hold seminars for both sports on football and basketball to help local women understand the games.

While at Pope, I got involved in soccer refereeing and rose to the position of head referee for the southeastern North Carolina region. I not only refereed, but also gave seminars on soccer officiating techniques throughout the region. I had the honor of being selected to referee the NC State Woman's High School East-West championship game in Greensboro, NC in 1992.

Dottie and I were both real estate brokers in Fayetteville. We took the opportunity to buy and renovate distressed homes and rent them out. I got out of the sales business and turned to rental management. In addition to our thirteen properties, I managed another forty properties for military members wanting to keep their homes and rent them out during their overseas assignments. Dottie became one of the top sellers for John Koenig Realtors in Fayetteville. In addition to managing 50 rentals, I bought a NOVUS Windshield Repair franchise and repaired automobile windshields until we moved to Boone.

While in Fayetteville, we invested as limited partners in Outback Steak House. As such, through a friend, we had the opportunity to accompany the outstanding Outback managers-of-the-year on an all-expenses-paid two-week trip to Australia. We were fortunate enough to take many cruises throughout the Caribbean, Alaska, and the capitals of all the Baltic countries including Saint Petersburg, Russia. We also had the opportunity to cruise the Mediterranean when Rob was assigned to Germany.

Also in Fayetteville, I took another risk and tried my hand at acting, singing, and dancing. We had two well-known playhouses in Fayetteville. The first was the 300 seat Fort Bragg Playhouse, and the Fayetteville Little Theatre, later renamed the Cape Fear Regional Theatre. I got my family, including our cocker Spaniel "Tuffy," involved in several productions. Family members were in the casts of *Carousel, Pajama Game, Jesus Christ Superstar, Guys and Dolls*, and *Camelot*. I was involved in many more, usually cast as the heavy, such as Mr. Bascomb in *Carousel*, Herr Detwiler in *The Sound of Music*, the Commissar in *Fiddler On The Roof*, Lt. Brannagan in *Guys and Dolls*, Mr. Bratt in *How To Succeed in Business Without Really Trying*, Thomas McKean in *1776*, a High Priest in *Jesus Christ Superstar*, Mame's first boyfriend in *Mame*, The Mayor in *Inherit The Wind*, and The Geneva Man in *Stalag 17*. I was a cast member in many other productions.

The directors brought in many well-known professional actors for the lead roles. Some of them I can remember included Joe Namath(quarterback NY Jets), Carl Anderson (played Judas in *Jesus Christ Superstar* movie), John Davidson (actor, singer, and game show host), Aileen Quinn (played the title role in the movie *Annie*), Ed Dennehy (Brian Dennehy's brother), and Noel Harrison (Rex Harrison's son).

When we took Rob to ASU, the only decent hotel in town had doubled their rates, since all parents were bringing their returning students, or as in our case, visiting ASU for the first time. This angered us in that we knew we would be coming here for at least the next four years. As realtors, we set out to find an investment home in Boone, and we were successful. We found a FISBO, "for sale by owner," and purchased it. Rob lived in it for his last three years and rented out rooms to other athletes and the downstairs apartment to a recent female graduate of ASU who worked at a local bank. I still have contact with her and her husband. When Rob graduated, we came to Boone and picked up all the beer cans on the .83 acre lot, took down the girlie posters and racecar photos, and decided to make it our summer home.

We moved to Boone permanently in 1997, having greatly increased the square footage by expanding the living room area, the kitchen, and adding a master bedroom suite. Later we added a sunroom and enlarged deck.

Upon Rob's graduation with three full majors, he was offered a job with the large BB&T banking institution. During his training, the Air Force called and offered him a flying slot through the Officer Training program (OTS). To quote Rob, "Dad I can always be a banker, but this is the only shot of becoming a pilot." This shocked us because he had never expressed an interest in the Air Force or flying.

Rick, on the other hand, always wanted to be a pilot, and rose to a high position in the UNC Chapel Hill ROTC program, not a particularly popular group on the liberal campus. He was the only one to gain a pilot slot and was commissioned a Second Lieutenant in the USAF. We are so proud of both boys as they each achieved their Master's degrees and retired as Air Force pilots and Lt. Colonels.

Retirement life in Boone was great. We became involved in the Boone United Methodist Church, The YOSEF Club, (an athletic scholarship and booster group for Appalachian State University), a tennis group, and were volunteers at the local hospital. We had season tickets to the athletic games and traveled to away games and conference championship tournaments. We even traveled to Michigan to watch our tiny team beat the fifth-ranked NCAA Michigan Wolverine football team in 2007. We went to the three national championship football games where ASU won the NCAA Championship division in 2007, 2008, and 2009.

We were very involved in the church, serving on many committees. Our church built a new beautiful structure and relocated in 2000. We

Bob and Dottie Reneau

were joint chairmen of the evangelism committee, and started several programs, including the parking lot hosts, where we served as greeters. Dottie had a special spot where she would be greeting arriving folks each Sunday rain, snow, or shine.

Dottie loved gardening and we (mostly Dottie) landscaped and built gardens all over our .83-acre very steep lot. We added a large sunroom and greatly enlarged our decks. It made our home feel like a large tree house surrounded by Dottie's little "birdies" as she called them.

Our twin grandsons Noah and Josh were born in Boone just before Rob's family left for an Air Force tour to England, followed by a tour in Germany. We missed having them around, but it gave us many opportunities to travel back to Europe. In our travels, we spent time with Rick's family in Texas, yet were overjoyed when he was assigned to Goldsboro, NC. They later moved to the fairly-close Atlanta, when he flew with the airlines. We continued to enjoy traveling and especially cruising. We visited all the Scandinavian countries and Russia. We also cruised to Alaska.

By this time, we had lost Dottie's parents and brother and my parents and brother. Life went on in our newly-found paradise, but unfortunately, God decided he needed Dottie more than I did and chose to bring her home in March of 2010. She died of complications from Non-Hodgkin's Lymphoma. After her passing, our church installed a wrought iron bench and a plaque stating "Dottie's Bench" at the spot where she stood while greeting service attendees.

As of this writing, it's been eight long and lonely years, but I have managed to find some highlights. I continue to be involved at the church and volunteering at the hospital. I have many dear friends. Dottie had signed me up for art lessons several years ago and I have been painting in oil since then (call me Grandpa Moses). I have also started writing (talk about a risk-taker). This memoir serves as a first semi-professional attempt.

I have met many new friends including some lovely ladies. Having been married to Dottie for 43 years, I have become quite spoiled in that area. At my age, I probably will not re-marry. Things could change in the next years or so, and I might be able to cut down on the driving radius. I still want to travel, but will limit it to flying.

Speaking of flying, as one of the original AC-130 pilots, I am to be the keynote speaker at the national AC-130 convention October 2018 in Dayton, Ohio, at the Air Force Museum. I have already purchased my plane tickets.

One of the neatest things about this trip is that our original aircraft, AF541626, which was the only one we had for the first eight months of 1968 and which we flew every night over Laos and Vietnam, is mothballed at the Wright-Patterson Museum, Wright-Pattern AFB, Dayton, Ohio. The museum officials there have agreed to unseal it for me to go aboard her. I look forward to reuniting with that grand old lady with whom I shared some of the "Riskiest, Scariest, and Most Rewarding nights of my life.

Our original aircraft, AF541626, mothballed at the
National Museum of the United States Air Force, Wright-Patterson AFB,
Dayton, Ohio

FOLLOW-ON RISK-TAKERS

I wrote this book for my Prodigy and pray they enjoy their lives as much as I have mine.

Children: Cindy, Karen, Rob, and Rick

Grandchildren: Erin, Bridgette, Kyle, Dylan, Beau, Hailey, Mariah, Jake, Noah, Joshua, and Riley

Great Grandchildren: Brielle, Deklan, Brandon, Easton, and Dawson

ABOUT THE AUTHOR

Air Force Lieutenant Colonel (ret) Bob Reneau, the risk-taker, was born September 22, 1937, in Watonga, Oklahoma. His father, a Methodist pastor and unarmed Army chaplain, voluntarily went ashore on Omaha Beach during that invasion. A mine blew his landing craft out of the water. His mother was a Smith college graduate and social worker in the Boston, Massachusetts, urban community. She too, was a risk-taker who married a poor preacher, joining him in his ministry in Oklahoma during the Depression and the Dust Bowl.

Bob attended Southern Methodist University on a swimming and diving scholarship, graduating in 1959, after winning three Southwest Conference swimming championships. He received a Regular Air Force Commission as a Distinguished Graduate. As such, he served as a cadet wing commander.

Bob attended flying school with the first graduates of the Air Force Academy. He served in many countries, on many bases, and in almost all the major Air Force Commands: TAC, PACAF, Systems Command, Vietnam, USAFE, SAC, and MAC. He logged more than 8,000 flying hours in the A, B, C, E, and H models of the C-130, including the JC, RC, and AC versions.

Bob Reneau

Col Reneau was one of the six original pilots in the AC-130 program, stationed at Ubon, Thailand, from April 1968 to April 1969.

Following his gunship tour, Bob served in numerous covert and special operations assignments. He served his rated supplement tour on staff of the SR-71 8th Strategic Reconnaissance Wing and the SAC Inspector General's Team.

Bob's genetic heritage obviously led him to a personality and career that is documented in this memoir. His ventures resulted in worldwide travel, assignments, and missions, which led to decorations. Among those he was awarded: The Silver Star, The Distinguished Flying Cross,

The Vietnamese Cross of Gallantry with Bronze Star, twelve Air Medals, two Meritorious Service Medals, and numerous other decorations.

Bob now resides in Boone, North Carolina, home of the Appalachian State University Mountaineers, where he is completing his book, *SPECTRE 07, Memoir of a Risk-Taker.*

Made in the USA
Columbia, SC
09 February 2019